MW00949304

It All Began With Jesus

year 4

A publication of:
Hills of Grace Fellowship
330 E. Anamosa
Rapid City, SD 57701

How to use this book…

This is a book that is designed for you to read one chapter a day through the bible for an entire year. You will not read the entire bible in this year of this study, but yo will read entire books of the bible, reflect upon them with daily questions, all whil seeing how big moments happen when we pray to the God of the universe.

We truly want you to know Him--Jesus. There are hints of Jesus all throughout the Old Testament and throughout the New Testament. That's because God planned for Jesus from before the foundation of the world. He gave hints of the need for Jesus and prophecies of His coming all through time. IN this study, we hope that you see the need for all of mankind to know Jesus and in your study, and you grow to become more like Him

This book is also designed to start whenever you wish to start, but on December 1st, you will STOP right where you are at and head to the back of the book, where you will find the ADVENT section.
We have 25 days specifically chosen to set your heart on remembering the impact and significance of the birth of our Lord. We end this on Christmas Day.

On December 26th, you will pick up where you left off prior to Advent. The same thing will happen with the start of Lent, whenever that falls in the year you are studying this.

Ash Wednesday is where Lent begins and this study will take you through 47 days which are specifically designed to set your heart on remembering the impact and significance of the death and resurrection of our Lord. We end this on Easter.

We hope this study helps challenge your faith in the most important ways. That when you finish this study, you know more about the faith you have claimed, and that you've made changes in the way you follow Him, and you're ready to impact the world in His name.

The Book of Matthrew

Read Matthew 1 **Date** _____

Recap:

- We get a detailed genealogy of Jesus that strengthens the foretelling that the Messiah would be a descendant of King David.

- Women are mentioned in the genealogy too, signaling that God had a plan for women and gentiles to be in his salvation plan.

What stands out to you in this chapter?

Where do you see God in this chapter?

How have you been challenged while reading this chapter?

Any lingering thoughts or questions following the reading?

Read Matthew 2   **Date** _____

Recap:

- King Herod was deeply disturbed that wise men were worshiping a baby, called the "King of the Jews."

- Herod was so worried about this baby, that he gave orders to massacre all male children in and around Bethlehem who were two years old or younger.

- When Herod eventually died, an angel of the Lord appeared to Joseph, letting him know that the coast was clear to bring his family back to the land of Israel.

What stands out to you in this chapter?

Where do you see God in this chapter?

How have you been challenged while reading this chapter?

Any lingering thoughts or questions following the reading?

ead Matthew 3   **Date** _____

ecap:

- John the Baptist comes on the scene and begins to teach the people to repent, as the kingdom of heaven is at hand.

- John baptized people with water for repentance.

- John let others know that the one who will come after him (Jesus), will be more powerful than him.

What stands out to you in this chapter?

Where do you see God in this chapter?

How have you been challenged while reading this chapter?

Any lingering thoughts or questions following the reading?

Read Matthew 4   **Date** _____

Recap:

- Jesus was tempted by the devil, so he fasted for 40 days and 40 nights in the wilderness.
- Jesus told the devil that it is written, "Do not test the Lord your God."
- John gets arrested.
- We meet the first disciples: Peter, Andrew, James, and John.
- Large crowds gather as Jesus heals.

What stands out to you in this chapter?

Where do you see God in this chapter?

How have you been challenged while reading this chapter?

Any lingering thoughts or questions following the reading?

Read Matthew 5   **Date** _____

Recap:

- The sermon on the mount begins with the Beatitudes.

- Believers are the salt of the earth and the light of the world.

- We learn that when you hate someone, you murder them in your heart

- God tells us to love our enemies

What stands out to you in this chapter?

Where do you see God in this chapter?

How have you been challenged while reading this chapter?

Any lingering thoughts or questions following the reading?

Read Matthew 6   **Date** _____

Recap:

- Don't sound a trumpet when you give.

- We are taught how to pray with the Lord's prayer.

- When we fast spiritually, we don't flaunt it.

- Verses 25-34 give us the Cure for Anxiety.

What stands out to you in this chapter?

Where do you see God in this chapter?

How have you been challenged while reading this chapter?

Any lingering thoughts or questions following the reading?

Read Matthew 7   **Date** _____

Recap:

- We learn how to Judge others by taking the plank out of our own eye, so we can clearly see what is going on with our brother in Christ. (So YES! We make judgments. Let's just do it biblically)

- Entering the kingdom of heaven is going to be through a narrow gate.

- False prophets are going to be all over, but may not look false at first glance.

- Jesus declares the need for a strong Christian foundation. (Build a house upon a rock analogy)

What stands out to you in this chapter?

Where do you see God in this chapter?

How have you been challenged while reading this chapter?

Any lingering thoughts or questions following the reading?

Read Matthew 8   **Date** _____

Recap:

- Jesus heals a man and tells him not to tell anyone, but to show his priest; in order to testify to the miracle that Jesus had just performed.

- Jesus heals Peter's mother-in-law.

- Jesus casts out demons.

What stands out to you in this chapter?

Where do you see God in this chapter?

How have you been challenged while reading this chapter?

Any lingering thoughts or questions following the reading?

Read Matthew 9   **Date** _____

Recap:

- Jesus teaches on the forgiving of sins and gets accused of blasphemy.
- Matthew joins the discipleship squad.
- Jesus foretells his death in a question that comes up about fasting.

What stands out to you in this chapter?

Where do you see God in this chapter?

How have you been challenged while reading this chapter?

Any lingering thoughts or questions following the reading?

Read Matthew 10   **Date** _____

Recap:

- Jesus commissions the twelve with very clear instructions beginning in verse 5.

- Those sending out WILL be persecuted.

- Do not fear man; fear God.

- Do not be afraid to acknowledge Christ before men; as Christ will acknowledge us before His father in heaven.

What stands out to you in this chapter?

Where do you see God in this chapter?

How have you been challenged while reading this chapter?

Any lingering thoughts or questions following the reading?

Read Matthew 11   **Date** _____

Recap:

- Jesus sent his 12 out to share the gospel, Jesus began to preach in the disciples' towns.
- Despite the miracles Jesus performed, he began to notice unrepented cities and called them out by name.
- Jesus calls all who are weary and burdened to come to Him to receive rest.

What stands out to you in this chapter?

Where do you see God in this chapter?

How have you been challenged while reading this chapter?

Any lingering thoughts or questions following the reading?

Read Matthew 12   **Date** _____

Recap:

- We get a lesson on the Sabbath, as Jesus and his disciples pass through a fiel and get accused of doing something unlawful.
- We find out if Jesus should be healing on the Sabbath.
- We learn that a good tree bears fruit and what it means.

What stands out to you in this chapter?

Where do you see God in this chapter?

How have you been challenged while reading this chapter?

Any lingering thoughts or questions following the reading?

Read Matthew 13   **Date** _____

Recap:

- Jesus explains why he uses parables; as his information is for them to know and not for everyone to understand until it's time.

- Jesus speaks on the parable of the Sower, Wheat and the Weeds, Mustard Seed, and a few more in this chapter.

- Jesus returned to his hometown of Nazareth and his teaching was not welcomed.

What stands out to you in this chapter?

Where do you see God in this chapter?

How have you been challenged while reading this chapter?

Any lingering thoughts or questions following the reading?

Read Matthew 14   **Date** _____

Recap:

- John the baptist is martyred.

- Jesus turns 5 loaves of bread and two fish to feed 5000 people.

- Jesus walks on water and we witness Peter being spooked by the wind and falling into the water.

What stands out to you in this chapter?

Where do you see God in this chapter?

How have you been challenged while reading this chapter?

Any lingering thoughts or questions following the reading?

Read Matthew 15   **Date** _____

Recap:

- Jesus is teaching that the authority of scriptures trumps all human traditions.

- We learn that from the heart comes evil thoughts, murders, adulteries, sexual immoralities, thefts, false testimonies, and blasphemies. So don't trust your heart!

- Jesus feeds 4,000 with 7 loaves of bread and a few small fish.

What stands out to you in this chapter?

Where do you see God in this chapter?

How have you been challenged while reading this chapter?

Any lingering thoughts or questions following the reading?

Read Matthew 16   **Date** _____

Recap:

- Jesus is annoyed that the disciples didn't have any bread and they were wondering where it was going to come from; even though they know very well that Jesus can turn a few loaves into many loaves.

- He lets his disciples know that he will be killed, but he will rise from the dead.

- Christians are supposed to pick up their cross and follow Jesus.

What stands out to you in this chapter?

Where do you see God in this chapter?

How have you been challenged while reading this chapter?

Any lingering thoughts or questions following the reading?

Read Matthew 17   **Date** _____

Recap:

- The Transfiguration took place: where Jesus turned completely white as light and was talking to Elijah and Moses.

- The disciples were freaking out, but Jesus told them to not be afraid.

- Jesus mentions his upcoming death for the 4th time. (Matthew 17:12, 12:40, 16:21, and 17:23)

What stands out to you in this chapter?

Where do you see God in this chapter?

How have you been challenged while reading this chapter?

Any lingering thoughts or questions following the reading?

Read Matthew 18   **Date** _____

Recap:

- Jesus teaches the adults to convert and humble themselves like children, in order to see the kingdom of God.

- The parable of the lost sheep and the 99 sheep is laid out.

- Church Discipline 101: Bring a sin to a brother. If he doesn't listen, bring two or three witnesses, and if that doesn't cause him to see the light and repent, bring him before the entire church body. And if no repentance; we are to treat them as a non believer or a tax collector in hopes they repent.

What stands out to you in this chapter?

Where do you see God in this chapter?

How have you been challenged while reading this chapter?

Any lingering thoughts or questions following the reading?

Read Matthew 19   **Date** _____

Recap:

- When two people are married, they are no longer two, but one flesh.

- Jesus says, "Whoever divorces his wife, except for sexual immorality, and marries another, commits adultery."

- Jesus encounters the rich young ruler and asks him to give his belongings to the poor and follow Him. His love for his belongings was too much, so he didn't follow Jesus' advice.

What stands out to you in this chapter?

Where do you see God in this chapter?

How have you been challenged while reading this chapter?

Any lingering thoughts or questions following the reading?

Read Matthew 20   **Date** _____

Recap:

- Jesus walks us through the parable of the Vineyard Worker, where all receive the same pay, but did not all do the same work, showing them to only worry about their own work and their own pay.

- Jesus tells the disciples again in verse 18, that he'll be killed.

- Jesus heals two blind men after leaving Jericho.

What stands out to you in this chapter?

Where do you see God in this chapter?

How have you been challenged while reading this chapter?

Any lingering thoughts or questions following the reading?

Read Matthew 21   **Date** _____

Recap:

- Jesus makes his public entry to Jerusalem (Palm Sunday)
- The people hooted and hollered in favor of him, as they thought he was coming to save them from government tyranny.
- Jesus says, "If you believe, you will receive whatever you ask for in prayer."

What stands out to you in this chapter?

Where do you see God in this chapter?

How have you been challenged while reading this chapter?

Any lingering thoughts or questions following the reading?

Read Matthew 22   **Date** _____

Recap:

- Jesus says, "Give back to Caesar the things that are Caesar's, and to God the things that are God's." (vs 22)

- Jesus teaches that there will be no marriage in heaven.

- We are to love your Lord your God with all your heart, with all your soul, and with all your mind. (What is distracting us from living out verse 37)

What stands out to you in this chapter?

Where do you see God in this chapter?

How have you been challenged while reading this chapter?

Any lingering thoughts or questions following the reading?

ead Matthew 23   **Date** _____

ecap:

- We are taught to not call anyone on earth father (Lord), as you only have one Father in heaven.

- A lot of "woe to you's" are mentioned here. (Discuss them amongst each other)

- Jesus expresses his disappointment in Jerusalem, the town who kills the prophets and stones who are sent to them.

What stands out to you in this chapter?

Where do you see God in this chapter?

How have you been challenged while reading this chapter?

Any lingering thoughts or questions following the reading?

Read Matthew 24   **Date** _____

Recap:

- Jesus warns us that false teachers will come and tell them that they are the messiah and will deceive many.

- We are told by Jesus that we, as believers, will be hated because of His name.

- We get a glimpse of what it will be like when Christ returns in verses 29-31

- No one knows the day or the hour of His return.

What stands out to you in this chapter?

Where do you see God in this chapter?

How have you been challenged while reading this chapter?

Any lingering thoughts or questions following the reading?

Read Matthew 25   **Date** _____

Recap:

- We learn in the Parable of the Talents that if you can be faithful with a few things, you could be put in charge of many things.

- Jesus reminds us that whatever we do for the least of "these" we have done unto him or not unto him in verses 35-46.

What stands out to you in this chapter?

Where do you see God in this chapter?

How have you been challenged while reading this chapter?

Any lingering thoughts or questions following the reading?

Read Matthew 26   **Date** _____

Recap:

- Jesus is betrayed by Judas for thirty pieces of silver.

- Jesus has a passover meal with his disciples and teaches them how and why to do communion.

- Jesus surprises Peter when he tells him that he will betray Him three times.

What stands out to you in this chapter?

Where do you see God in this chapter?

How have you been challenged while reading this chapter?

Any lingering thoughts or questions following the reading?

Read Matthew 27   **Date** _____

Recap:

- Judas returns the silver, grieves over betraying Jesus, and hangs himself.
- The crowd chooses Jesus to crucify over Barabbas (who was the true criminal).
- Jesus is crucified. The thief on the cross next to Jesus is saved by Jesus.
- Jesus dies and the tomb is closely guarded, as well as a giant stone placed in front of the entry, so no one can get into where Jesus was laid.

What stands out to you in this chapter?

Where do you see God in this chapter?

How have you been challenged while reading this chapter?

Any lingering thoughts or questions following the reading?

Read Matthew 28   **Date** _____

Recap:

- Mary Magdalene and the other Mary went to the tomb in the morning and they met an angel, who told them not to be afraid, but Jesus was not there.
- Jesus appears to the women, then the disciples.
- We are commissioned to go into all the nations, baptizing new believers in the name of The Father, The Son, and The Holy Spirit.

What stands out to you in this chapter?

Where do you see God in this chapter?

How have you been challenged while reading this chapter?

Any lingering thoughts or questions following the reading?

The Book of Genesis

Read Genesis 1   **Date** _____

Recap:

- In the beginning, God created....."The Big Bang!!!!"
- God creates light, darkness, water, the sky, land and sea creatures; and so much more!
- God created man in His own image/He created them male and female

What stands out to you in this chapter?

Where do you see God in this chapter?

How have you been challenged while reading this chapter?

Any lingering thoughts or questions following the reading?

Read Genesis 2   **Date** _____

Recap:

- Heaven and Earth and the Garden of Eden are created.

- God created Eve out of the rib of Adam.

- Man leaves his father and mother and bonds with his wife, and they become one flesh.

What stands out to you in this chapter?

Where do you see God in this chapter?

How have you been challenged while reading this chapter?

Any lingering thoughts or questions following the reading?

Read Genesis 3   **Date** _____

Recap:

- The serpent comes on the scene and confuses Eve and tricks her into eating from the tree.
- We see how quickly we know when we're guilty and ashamed and hide, as Adam and Eve did when God wanted to talk about them eating from the tree.
- We learn of the consequences from them eating from the tree.

What stands out to you in this chapter?

Where do you see God in this chapter?

How have you been challenged while reading this chapter?

Any lingering thoughts or questions following the reading?

Read Genesis 4   **Date** _____

Recap:

- Adam and Eve are intimate, and as a result, conceive Cain and Abel.

- When the boys were older, Cain attacked Abel and killed him with a rock.

- The Lord tells Cain that he now cursed for what he has done.

What stands out to you in this chapter?

Where do you see God in this chapter?

How have you been challenged while reading this chapter?

Any lingering thoughts or questions following the reading?

Read Genesis 5   **Date** _____

Recap:

- Adam was 130 years old when he fathered a son in his likeness (Seth)
- Adam lived 800 years after the birth of Seth and fathered many children.
- We read about Adam's genealogy in more detail with his children.

What stands out to you in this chapter?

Where do you see God in this chapter?

How have you been challenged while reading this chapter?

Any lingering thoughts or questions following the reading?

Read Genesis 6   **Date** _____

Recap:

- The Lord saw that man's wickedness was widespread and he regretted that he had made man on the earth at all.

- Noah found favor with the Lord, and the Lord commissioned Noah to make an ark, which would save some people and creatures, when God began to flood the earth.

What stands out to you in this chapter?

Where do you see God in this chapter?

How have you been challenged while reading this chapter?

Any lingering thoughts or questions following the reading?

ead Genesis 7   **Date** _____

ecap:

- Noah and his family entered the ark and the Lord instructed him to take with him pairs of animals (beginning at verse 2)
- The Lord flooded the earth as rain fell on the earth for 40 days and 40 nights, allowing only those on the ark to survive.

What stands out to you in this chapter?

Where do you see God in this chapter?

How have you been challenged while reading this chapter?

Any lingering thoughts or questions following the reading?

Read Genesis 8   **Date** _____

Recap:

- God made it windy, and the water began to subside; ten months after the flood began.

- Noah sent out a raven, then a dove to see if there was dry land anywhere.

- Finally, the earth was dry and Noah was able to open the ark and let everyone out.

What stands out to you in this chapter?

Where do you see God in this chapter?

How have you been challenged while reading this chapter?

Any lingering thoughts or questions following the reading?

Read Genesis 9   **Date** _____

Recap:

- Noah is instructed by God to be fruitful and multiply the earth.

- God makes a covenant to never flood the earth again.

- Canaan will be cursed for his actions.

What stands out to you in this chapter?

Where do you see God in this chapter?

How have you been challenged while reading this chapter?

Any lingering thoughts or questions following the reading?

Read Genesis 10   **Date** _____

Recap:

- We get a list of Noah's sons and their descendants (Shem, Ham, and Japeth)

- They spread out over three large geographic areas.

- **Ham** is on the east side of the Red Sea (modern day Egypt, Sudan, and surrounding areas., while **Shem** inherited the land west of the Red sea modern day Yemen, Saudi Arabia, and surrounding areas), and **Japheth** was North of Shem and west of the Persian Gulf (modern day Italy, Greece, Iran, and surrounding areas).

What stands out to you in this chapter?

Where do you see God in this chapter?

How have you been challenged while reading this chapter?

Any lingering thoughts or questions following the reading?

ead Genesis 11:   **Date** _____

ecap:

- People in the world all had the same language, until Genesis 11:7.
- The genealogy here connects Noah's son Shem to Abram/Abraham, as well as Seth to Abram/Abraham.

Vhat stands out to you in this chapter?

Vhere do you see God in this chapter?

Iow have you been challenged while reading this chapter?

Any lingering thoughts or questions following the reading?

Read Genesis 12:   **Date** _____

Recap:

- Abram gets a call to leave all that he knew and follow the Lord on a mission

- Abram had his wife, Sarai pretend to be his sister, as he thought that would spare her life.

- Pharoah and his household was struck with several plagues.

What stands out to you in this chapter?

Where do you see God in this chapter?

How have you been challenged while reading this chapter?

Any lingering thoughts or questions following the reading?

Read Genesis 13:   **Date** _____

Recap:

- In verse 4, Abram's returned where God first spoke to him (Negev), and it was also the first time he has called on the name of the Lord since he left Canaan for Egypt.

- Lot was traveling with Abram and Sarai, and they decided to split in opposite directions.

What stands out to you in this chapter?

Where do you see God in this chapter?

How have you been challenged while reading this chapter?

Any lingering thoughts or questions following the reading?

Read Genesis 14:   **Date** _____

Recap:

- Lot was being held captive, so Abram with his men attacked them at night and brought back all the goods and Lot and his goods, as well as the women and the other people.

- Melchizedek, the King of Salem blessed Abram and praised God; and Abram gave him a tenth of everything.

What stands out to you in this chapter?

Where do you see God in this chapter?

How have you been challenged while reading this chapter?

Any lingering thoughts or questions following the reading?

ead Genesis 15:   **Date** _____

ecap:

- Abram gets a vision from God and is told that he'll be an heir from his own body.
- The Lord also revealed to Abram what would happen in the next 430 years (through Exodus 12).

What stands out to you in this chapter?

Where do you see God in this chapter?

How have you been challenged while reading this chapter?

Any lingering thoughts or questions following the reading?

Read Genesis 16:   **Date** _____

Recap:

- Sarai gave Hagar, her Egyptian slave, to her husband Abram to help him bea
  a child; and Hagar became pregnant.

- Hagar was being mistreated by Sarai later on, and Hagar ran away.

- The Lord came to Hagar and convinced her to return and be mistreated, but
  she would be rewarded with more offspring; specifically Ishmael.

What stands out to you in this chapter?

Where do you see God in this chapter?

How have you been challenged while reading this chapter?

Any lingering thoughts or questions following the reading?

Read Genesis 17:   **Date** _____

Recap:

- The Lord appeared to Abram when he was 99 years old and told him that he would be the father of many nations.

- The Lord makes a covenant with Abram and his future male offsprings and slaves will be circumcised.

- The Lord changes Sarai's name to Sarah and Abram's name to Abraham; and he informs them that Sarah will bear a son (Isaac).

What stands out to you in this chapter?

Where do you see God in this chapter?

How have you been challenged while reading this chapter?

Any lingering thoughts or questions following the reading?

Read Genesis 18:   **Date** _____

Recap:

- The Lord appeared to Abraham and told him that he'd return in a year's time and they would have a baby. Sarah laughed, as she overheard.

- Sarah didn't believe she could have a baby at her old age.

- The Lord and Abraham have a conversation regarding whether or not Sodom and Gammorah would be destroyed.

What stands out to you in this chapter?

Where do you see God in this chapter?

How have you been challenged while reading this chapter?

Any lingering thoughts or questions following the reading?

ead Genesis 19:   **Date** _____

ecap:

- Lot offers up his two virgin daughters to satisfy the desires of the men.

- The angels tell Lot to get all his loved ones out, as the place is about to be destroyed.

- The family didn't leave, but were still spared by the Lord.

What stands out to you in this chapter?

Where do you see God in this chapter?

How have you been challenged while reading this chapter?

Any lingering thoughts or questions following the reading?

Read Genesis 20: **Date** _____

Recap:

- God came to Abimelech in a dream and told him that he was going to die because he took Sarah.

- God told him to return Sarah to Abraham.

- Abraham prayed and God healed Abimelech, his wife, and his female slaves so that they could bear children.

What stands out to you in this chapter?

Where do you see God in this chapter?

How have you been challenged while reading this chapter?

Any lingering thoughts or questions following the reading?

Read Genesis 21:   **Date** _____

Recap:

- Isaac was born when Abraham was 100 years old.

- Ishmael was sent away for mocking/persecuting Isaac, which was difficult for Abraham.

What stands out to you in this chapter?

Where do you see God in this chapter?

How have you been challenged while reading this chapter?

Any lingering thoughts or questions following the reading?

Read Genesis 22:   **Date** _____

Recap:

- The Lord tells Abraham to take Isaac to a mountain and he'll give him more instructions.
- Abraham built an altar, bound Isaac and placed him on top of the wood and was about to stab his son, as a sacrifice.
- The Lord stopped him and Isaac was spared.

What stands out to you in this chapter?

Where do you see God in this chapter?

How have you been challenged while reading this chapter?

Any lingering thoughts or questions following the reading?

Read Genesis 23:   **Date** _____

Recap:

- Sarah died at the ripe old age of 127.

- Abraham negotiated a price to buy land from Ephron for 400 shekels of silver, to bury his dead.

What stands out to you in this chapter?

Where do you see God in this chapter?

How have you been challenged while reading this chapter?

Any lingering thoughts or questions following the reading?

Read Genesis 24:   **Date** _____

Recap:

- Abraham, commissions his oldest servant to find a suitable wife for his son Isaac.

- The servant embarks on his journey to Mesopotamia and prays for God's guidance, asking for a specific sign to identify the right woman for Isaac.

- Recognizing that God has led him to the right woman, the servant bows and worships the Lord, acknowledging His providence and faithfulness.

- Rebekah willingly accepts the proposal and accompanies the servant back to Canaan, where she eventually becomes Isaac's wife, continuing the lineage of God's chosen people.

What stands out to you in this chapter?

Where do you see God in this chapter?

How have you been challenged while reading this chapter?

Any lingering thoughts or questions following the reading?

Read Genesis 25:   **Date** _____

Recap:

- Abraham, commissions his oldest servant to find a suitable wife for his son Isaac.

- The servant embarks on his journey to Mesopotamia and prays for God's guidance, asking for a specific sign to identify the right woman for Isaac.

- Recognizing that God has led him to the right woman, the servant bows and worships the Lord, acknowledging His providence and faithfulness.

- Rebekah willingly accepts the proposal and accompanies the servant back to Canaan, where she eventually becomes Isaac's wife, continuing the lineage of God's chosen people.

What stands out to you in this chapter?

Where do you see God in this chapter?

How have you been challenged while reading this chapter?

Any lingering thoughts or questions following the reading?

Read Genesis 26:   **Date** _____

Recap:

- Isaac faces a famine in the land, similar to what his father Abraham encountered.

- God instructs Isaac not to go to Egypt but to remain in Gerar.

- Out of fear for his life, Isaac lies to Abimelech, the king of Gerar, claiming that his wife Rebekah is his sister, just as Abraham did with Sarah.

- Isaac digs new wells, but the Philistines dispute over them.

- Eventually, he moves away from Gerar and settles in Beersheba, where God reaffirms His promise to bless him and his descendants.

- Abimelech, recognizing God's favor on Isaac, seeks a covenant of peace with him to avoid any future conflicts.

What stands out to you in this chapter?

Where do you see God in this chapter?

How have you been challenged while reading this chapter?

Any lingering thoughts or questions following the reading?

ead Genesis 27:   **Date** _____

ecap:

- Isaac intends on blessing Esau, his oldest son, but Rebekah comes up with a plan to have Jacob receive the blessing instead.
- Esau returns from hunting and discovers Jacob's deception. He is devastated and begs for a blessing from his father.
- Isaac realizes the deception but admits that Jacob has already received the blessing meant for Esau, and it cannot be revoked.
- Esau becomes furious and vows to kill Jacob after their father's death, prompting Rebekah to send Jacob away to her brother Laban's house for safety and to find a wife from their family.

What stands out to you in this chapter?

Where do you see God in this chapter?

How have you been challenged while reading this chapter?

Any lingering thoughts or questions following the reading?

Read Genesis 28:   **Date** _____

Recap:

- Fleeing from his brother Esau's anger, Jacob travels toward Haran, where his mother's family resides.

- God reaffirms the Abrahamic covenant with Jacob, promising him numerous descendants and the land on which he lies.

- Moved by the encounter with God in his dream, Jacob makes a vow, promising that if God watches over him, provides for him, and brings him safely back to his father's house, he will worship God and give a tenth of all he possesses to Him.

- Moved by the encounter with God in his dream, Jacob makes a vow, promising that if God watches over him, provides for him, and brings him safely back to his father's house, he will worship God and give a tenth of all he possesses to Him.

What stands out to you in this chapter?

Where do you see God in this chapter?

How have you been challenged while reading this chapter?

Any lingering thoughts or questions following the reading?

Read Genesis 29:   **Date** _____

Recap:

- When Rachel arrives at the well, Jacob rolls the stone from the well's mouth and waters Laban's sheep, revealing himself as a relative.

- Jacob stays with Laban, and after a month, Laban offers him to work for wages. Jacob agrees to work for seven years to marry Rachel, whom he loves deeply.

- After the seven years are completed, Jacob requests Rachel's hand in marriage, but Laban deceives him and substitutes his older daughter, Leah, for Rachel on the wedding night.

- Jacob discovers the deception in the morning but agrees to work another seven years to marry Rachel as well, as he deeply desires her.

What stands out to you in this chapter?

Where do you see God in this chapter?

How have you been challenged while reading this chapter?

Any lingering thoughts or questions following the reading?

Read Genesis 30:   **Date** _____

Recap:

- Rachel, seeing that her sister Leah has borne children to Jacob, becomes jealous and desperately longs for children of her own.

- Rachel, unable to bear children, takes matters into her own hands and gives her maidservant Bilhah to Jacob as a wife, following the custom of the time.

- Bilhah conceives and bears two sons on behalf of Rachel, Dan and Naphtali.

- Rachel desires the mandrakes, and Leah bargains with her, offering to let Jacob spend the night with her in exchange for the mandrakes.

- Later, God remembers Rachel's plea for children, and she conceives and bears a son named Joseph, expressing her gratitude for God's blessing.

What stands out to you in this chapter?

Where do you see God in this chapter?

How have you been challenged while reading this chapter?

Any lingering thoughts or questions following the reading?

ead Genesis 31:   **Date** _____

ecap:

- God instructs Jacob to return to the land of his fathers, promising to be with him and bless him.

- Jacob gathers his wives, children, and possessions secretly and leaves without informing Laban.

- Laban confronts Jacob, accusing him of deceitfully leaving and taking his daughters and grandchildren with him.

- The two men reach a covenant, setting up a heap of stones as a witness of their agreement not to harm each other.

- They part ways, and Laban returns to his land, while Jacob continues his journey back to the land of Canaan, where he is met by angels of God.

What stands out to you in this chapter?

Where do you see God in this chapter?

How have you been challenged while reading this chapter?

Any lingering thoughts or questions following the reading?

Read Genesis 32:   **Date** _____

Recap:

- Jacob, on his way back to Canaan, learns that Esau is coming to meet him with 400 men. Fearing for his safety and that of his family and possessions, Jacob becomes worried.

- Jacob sends his family and belongings across the Jabbok River, but he remains alone on the other side.

- During the night, a man wrestles with Jacob until daybreak. This "man" is often understood to be a theophany, an appearance of God in human form.

- The "man" blesses Jacob and renames him Israel, which means "struggles with God," signifying the transformative nature of the encounter.

- To Jacob's surprise, Esau runs to meet him, embraces him, and displays forgiveness and reconciliation. They part in peace, with Esau returning to Seir and Jacob settling in Succoth.

What stands out to you in this chapter?

Where do you see God in this chapter?

How have you been challenged while reading this chapter?

Any lingering thoughts or questions following the reading?

Read Genesis 33:   **Date** _____

Recap:

- As Jacob and his family draw near to Esau and his 400 men, Jacob arranges his family in order of importance, placing the maidservants and their children first, followed by Leah and her children, and Rachel and then Joseph.

- Jacob himself goes ahead of them, bowing to the ground seven times as a sign of humility and respect.

- When Esau sees Jacob approaching, he runs to meet him, embraces him, and weeps, characterizing forgiveness and genuine affection.

- Jacob presents a generous gift of livestock to Esau as a gesture of peace and reconciliation.

- Esau initially refuses the gift, stating that he has plenty, but Jacob insists that he accepts it as a sign of Jacob's desire for a peaceful relationship.

What stands out to you in this chapter?

Where do you see God in this chapter?

How have you been challenged while reading this chapter?

Any lingering thoughts or questions following the reading?

Read Genesis 34:   **Date** _____

Recap:

- Shechem, the son of Hamor, the ruler of Shechem, seizes Dinah and violates her.

- After the incident, Shechem becomes infatuated with Dinah and asks his father to arrange a marriage with her.

- Jacob's sons, Simeon and Levi, learn of their sister's violation and become furious with Shechem and his family.

- They plan to gain revenge by agreeing to the marriage proposal but demand that all the men of Shechem be circumcised first.

- While the men of Shechem are recovering from the circumcision, Simeon and Levi attack the city and kill every male, including Shechem and Hamor.

What stands out to you in this chapter?

Where do you see God in this chapter?

How have you been challenged while reading this chapter?

Any lingering thoughts or questions following the reading?

ead Genesis 35:   **Date** _____

ecap:

- God instructs Jacob to return to Bethel, where he had previously encountered God and made a vow (Genesis 28:10-22).

- Jacob commands his household to put away their foreign gods and purify themselves, preparing to meet God at Bethel.

- God appears to Jacob again, reaffirming the covenant He made with him and giving him the name "Israel," signifying a new phase in Jacob's life and identity as a man who wrestles with God.

- Rachel dies during childbirth.

- The birth of Benjamin adds to the number of Jacob's twelve sons, who will later become the heads of the twelve tribes of Israel.

- Isaac dies at the age of 180.

What stands out to you in this chapter?

Where do you see God in this chapter?

How have you been challenged while reading this chapter?

Any lingering thoughts or questions following the reading?

Read Genesis 36:   **Date** _____

Recap:

- The chapter lists the names of Esau's wives, sons, and grandsons, tracing the genealogy of the Edomite tribes that descended from him.

- Genesis 36 provides a list of Edomite chiefs, who ruled over various regions in Edom before the establishment of kings in Israel.

- The Edomite chiefs are listed alongside the kings who ruled Israel before the monarchy was established.

- The inclusion of this genealogy emphasizes the fulfillment of God's promises to Esau (Edom), the brother of Jacob (Israel). God had foretold that Esau's descendants would also become a great nation (Genesis 25:23).

What stands out to you in this chapter?

Where do you see God in this chapter?

How have you been challenged while reading this chapter?

Any lingering thoughts or questions following the reading?

Read Genesis 37:   **Date** _____

Recap:

- Joseph, being one of Jacob's favored sons, receives a special coat from his father, signifying his favored status.
- Joseph has two dreams in which he sees himself in a position of authority over his brothers and even his parents. He shares these dreams with his family.
- His brothers become envious and resentful of Joseph's dreams and his favored position, adding to the existing tension and rivalry among them.
- Joseph's brothers take his special coat, dip it in goat's blood, and present it to Jacob, deceiving him into believing that Joseph was killed by a wild animal.
- Jacob is deeply grieved by the apparent loss of his beloved son and mourns him.
- Meanwhile, Joseph is taken as a slave to Egypt, where he begins his journey that will eventually lead to his rise to power.

What stands out to you in this chapter?

Where do you see God in this chapter?

How have you been challenged while reading this chapter?

Any lingering thoughts or questions following the reading?

Read Genesis 38:   **Date** _____

Recap:

- Judah departs from his brothers and marries a Canaanite woman named Shua.

- They have three sons: Er, Onan, and Shelah. (Er marries Tamar)

- Er dies, but Onan refuses to marry Tamar; and chaos ensues.

- Judah becomes fearful that his youngest son, Shelah, might also die if married to Tamar, so he deceitfully sends her back to her father's house, promising her that Shelah will be given to her when he grows up.

- Tamar, feeling wronged and desperate for an heir, resorts to a deceptive plan to conceive from Judah. She disguises herself as a prostitute and waits for Judah by the road.

- Judah unwittingly sleeps with Tamar, thinking she is a prostitute. He leaves his staff, signet, and cord as collateral for payment.

What stands out to you in this chapter?

Where do you see God in this chapter?

How have you been challenged while reading this chapter?

Any lingering thoughts or questions following the reading?

ead Genesis 39:   **Date** _____

ecap:

- Joseph is taken to Egypt and sold to Potiphar, an officer of Pharaoh and captain of the guard.

- Despite being in a foreign land and a slave, Joseph remains faithful to God and gains favor in Potiphar's eyes.

- Potiphar entrusts Joseph with the management of his household, and everything under Joseph's care prospers.

- Joseph is thrown in prison, because Potiphar's wife tried to seduce him, but he turned her down, so she falsely accused him of assault.

- Even in prison, Joseph interpreted dreams and it becomes evident when he interprets the dreams of two fellow prisoners, the chief cupbearer and the chief baker.

What stands out to you in this chapter?

Where do you see God in this chapter?

How have you been challenged while reading this chapter?

Any lingering thoughts or questions following the reading?

Read Genesis 40:   **Date** _____

Recap:

- Joseph, with God's help, interprets two prisoners' dreams: he predicts that th
cupbearer will be restored to his former position, while the baker will be
executed in three days.

- As Joseph had foretold, the chief cupbearer is reinstated to his former
position, but the chief baker is executed, in accordance with the
interpretation of their dreams.

- Despite accurately interpreting the dreams of the cupbearer and baker,
Joseph's hopes for release are deferred, and he remains in prison for some
time longer.

What stands out to you in this chapter?

Where do you see God in this chapter?

How have you been challenged while reading this chapter?

Any lingering thoughts or questions following the reading?

Read Genesis 41:   **Date** _____

Recap:

- Joseph interprets the dreams of Pharaoh, revealing that God is foretelling seven years of abundance followed by seven years of severe famine.
- Impressed by Joseph's wisdom and understanding, Pharaoh appoints him as the second-in-command, giving him authority over all of Egypt.
- Pharaoh entrusts Joseph with the responsibility of storing surplus grain during the seven years of abundance to prepare for the upcoming famine.

What stands out to you in this chapter?

Where do you see God in this chapter?

How have you been challenged while reading this chapter?

Any lingering thoughts or questions following the reading?

Read Genesis 42:   **Date** _____

Recap:

- The famine affects Canaan, and Jacob sends his ten sons to Egypt to buy grain.

- Joseph, who is in charge of grain distribution in Egypt, recognizes his brother when they come to him but conceals his identity from them.

- Joseph accused his brothers of being spies and put them in custody for three days as a test of their integrity.

- Joseph instructs them to bring Benjamin as well as their youngest brother back to Egypt and warns them not to return unless they bring Benjamin with them.

- When the brothers discover the returned money from Joseph, they feel guilt and remorse for their past treatment of Joseph, seeing it as a consequence of their sins.

What stands out to you in this chapter?

Where do you see God in this chapter?

How have you been challenged while reading this chapter?

Any lingering thoughts or questions following the reading?

Read Genesis 43:   **Date** _____

Recap:

- Joseph is informed that his brothers have returned, and he orders the steward of his house to prepare a meal for them.

- When the brothers arrive, they present their gifts to Joseph, bow down before him, and express their concern about the returned money.

- Joseph assures them that God must have returned the money as a test of their integrity. He then reveals his knowledge of their family, specifically mentioning their younger brother, Benjamin.

- Joseph joins his brothers for the meal, still concealing his true identity from them.

What stands out to you in this chapter?

Where do you see God in this chapter?

How have you been challenged while reading this chapter?

Any lingering thoughts or questions following the reading?

Read Genesis 44:   **Date** _____

Recap:

- Joseph instructs his steward to fill his brothers' sacks with grain and secretly place his silver cup in Benjamin's sack.

- The brothers get accused of stealing the cup and immediately deny the accusation and declare that if the cup is found in any of their sacks, that person should become a slave to the Egyptian ruler.

- Judah offers himself as a substitute for Benjamin, proposing that he should become a slave in Benjamin's place to spare their elderly father from sorrow.

- Touched by Judah's heartfelt plea, Joseph can no longer contain his emotions and reveals his true identity to his brothers.

- Joseph urges his brothers to return to their father and bring him, along with their families, to Egypt, where they can live in the land of Goshen, close to him.

What stands out to you in this chapter?

Where do you see God in this chapter?

How have you been challenged while reading this chapter?

Any lingering thoughts or questions following the reading?

ead Genesis 45:   **Date** _____

ecap:

- Joseph reveals his true identity to his brothers, saying, "I am Joseph! Is my father still alive?" His brothers are stunned and terrified at this revelation.

- Joseph reassures his brothers, telling them not to be angry with themselves for selling him into slavery. He explains that God had a greater purpose in sending him to Egypt to preserve their lives during the famine.

- Joseph instructs his brothers to return to Canaan and bring their father Jacob and their families back to Egypt, where they can live in the land of Goshen and be provided for during the remaining years of famine.

- The brothers return to Canaan and tell their father Jacob the astonishing news that Joseph is alive and is the ruler of Egypt.

What stands out to you in this chapter?

Where do you see God in this chapter?

How have you been challenged while reading this chapter?

Any lingering thoughts or questions following the reading?

Read Genesis 46:   **Date** _____

Recap:

- God speaks to Jacob in a vision at Beersheba, assuring him not to fear going down to Egypt.

- God promises to make Jacob a great nation in Egypt and promises to bring hi descendants back to the land of Canaan.

- Jacob sets out for Egypt with all his descendants, including his sons, their wives, and their children, totaling seventy individuals.

- As Jacob and his family approach Egypt, Joseph prepares to meet his father after years of separation.

- Joseph presents himself to his father, and they have an emotional reunion, embracing each other and weeping.

What stands out to you in this chapter?

Where do you see God in this chapter?

How have you been challenged while reading this chapter?

Any lingering thoughts or questions following the reading?

ead Genesis 47:   **Date** _____

ecap:

- Pharaoh, impressed by Joseph's wisdom and administration, appoints him to oversee the distribution of food during the famine.

- The famine intensifies, and Joseph sells grain to the Egyptians and people from other nations who come to him seeking food. He also ensures that his family and father, Jacob, have enough provisions to survive the famine.

- As things get worse and people cannot afford to pay Joseph for his grain, he continues to provide for his family and the Egyptian population, skillfully managing the resources of the land during the seven years of famine.

- Jacob lives for seventeen years in Egypt, and he blesses Joseph's sons, Ephraim and Manasseh, adopting them as his own, with each becoming the head of a tribe in the future.

What stands out to you in this chapter?

Where do you see God in this chapter?

How have you been challenged while reading this chapter?

Any lingering thoughts or questions following the reading?

Read Genesis 48:   **Date** _____

Recap:

- Jacob adopts Ephraim and Manasseh as his own sons, giving them equal inheritance rights among their uncles, and blessing them as his own heirs.

- Jacob (who can barely see) deliberately crosses his arms when blessing the two boys, putting his right hand on Ephraim, the younger, and his left hand on Manasseh, the firstborn.

- When Joseph tries to correct the order, Jacob insists that he knows what he is doing, indicating God's sovereign choice in the reversal of blessings.

What stands out to you in this chapter?

Where do you see God in this chapter?

How have you been challenged while reading this chapter?

Any lingering thoughts or questions following the reading?

Read Genesis 49:   **Date** _____

Recap:

- Jacob gathers his sons and begins to prophesy over each one individually, speaking of their future roles and destinies.

- Jacob blesses Judah with the promise of kingship and leadership, foreshadowing the tribe's significance in the line of David and ultimately the Messiah.

- Jacob blesses Joseph with blessings of heaven and deep blessings of the breasts and womb, referring to the prosperity and blessings that will flow through Joseph's descendants.

- After blessing his twelve sons, Jacob provides instructions for his burial, asking to be buried with his ancestors in the cave of Machpelah, where Abraham and Sarah, Isaac and Rebekah, and Jacob's wife Leah are buried.

What stands out to you in this chapter?

Where do you see God in this chapter?

How have you been challenged while reading this chapter?

Any lingering thoughts or questions following the reading?

Read Genesis 50:   **Date** _____

Recap:

- After Jacob's death, Joseph and his brothers mourn their father for seventy days.

- Joseph seeks Pharaoh's permission to bury his father in Canaan, as Jacob had requested.

- Joseph reassures his brothers by showing compassion and forgiveness.

- He acknowledges that God had a greater purpose in their actions, using them to preserve life during the famine. He assures them that he will continue to provide for them and their families.

- Joseph lives to the age of 110 and sees his great-grandchildren born.

- Before his death, he makes the Israelites promise to take his bones back to the Promised Land when they leave Egypt, as a symbol of their faith in God's future fulfillment of His promise.

What stands out to you in this chapter?

Where do you see God in this chapter?

How have you been challenged while reading this chapter?

Any lingering thoughts or questions following the reading?

The Book of 1 Corinthians

ead 1 Corinthians 1   **Date** _____

ecap:

- Paul gives thanks, before he points out the divisions he knows about in the Church at Corinth.

- Paul emphasizes that true wisdom and righteousness come from God, and therefore, if anyone boasts, they should boast in the Lord.

- Paul explains that Christ has become to us wisdom from God, righteousness, sanctification, and redemption.

- Paul reminds the Corinthians that not many of them were wise, powerful, or noble in the world's eyes when they were called, but God chose the foolish and weak to shame the wise and strong.

- Paul encourages the Corinthians to glorify God in everything they do, acknowledging that it is by God's grace they are in Christ Jesus.

What stands out to you in this chapter?

Where do you see God in this chapter?

How have you been challenged while reading this chapter?

Any lingering thoughts or questions following the reading?

Read 1 Corinthians 2   **Date** _____

Recap:

- Paul explains that he preached with a demonstration of the Spirit's power so that their faith would not rest on human wisdom but on God's power.

- Paul explains that the hidden wisdom of God has been revealed to believers through the Spirit, who searches all things, even the deep things of God.

- Spiritual people are those who have the Spirit of God and can discern spiritual truths, while natural people cannot.

What stands out to you in this chapter?

Where do you see God in this chapter?

How have you been challenged while reading this chapter?

Any lingering thoughts or questions following the reading?

Read 1 Corinthians 3   **Date** _____

Recap:

- Paul addresses the Corinthians as infants in Christ, indicating that they are still spiritually immature and unable to handle solid spiritual food.

- Paul points out that there are divisions among the Corinthians, with some claiming allegiance to Paul and others to Apollos, causing jealousy and strife.

- Paul and Apollos are both servants of God, and they have different roles in planting and watering, but it is God who gives the growth.

What stands out to you in this chapter?

Where do you see God in this chapter?

How have you been challenged while reading this chapter?

Any lingering thoughts or questions following the reading?

Read 1 Corinthians 4   **Date** _____

Recap:

- Focus on the power of the Gospel rather than human wisdom and to imitate him as he imitates Christ.

- Paul's love and concern for the Corinthians shine through as he seeks their spiritual growth and warns against persisting in sin.

- The chapter serves as a reminder for believers to remain faithful to Christ and His teachings, humbly serving Him and one another.

What stands out to you in this chapter?

Where do you see God in this chapter?

How have you been challenged while reading this chapter?

Any lingering thoughts or questions following the reading?

Read 1 Corinthians 5   **Date** _____

Recap:

- Paul takes a strong stance against sin and immorality within the Church.
- He emphasizes the need for discipline and purity, urging the Corinthians to take action to remove sin from their midst.
- Paul's goal is not to condemn the individual but to bring about repentance and restoration through appropriate church discipline.
- This serves as a reminder to believers about the importance of holiness and accountability within the Christian community, ensuring that the Church remains a place of sincerity and truth, free from sin.

What stands out to you in this chapter?

Where do you see God in this chapter?

How have you been challenged while reading this chapter?

Any lingering thoughts or questions following the reading?

Read 1 Corinthians 6   **Date** _____

Recap:

- Paul addresses the issue of believers taking legal disputes before unbelievers and judges instead of settling them within the church.

- Paul criticizes the Corinthians for taking their disputes before the unrighteous pointing out that they should be able to resolve their issues among themselves.

- Paul emphasizes that our bodies are members of Christ and temples of the Holy Spirit, and we should, therefore, glorify God with our bodies.

What stands out to you in this chapter?

Where do you see God in this chapter?

How have you been challenged while reading this chapter?

Any lingering thoughts or questions following the reading?

Read 1 Corinthians 7   **Date** _____

Recap:

- Paul discusses the importance of marriage and the gift of celibacy, encouraging each person to embrace their God-given calling.

- Paul advises those who are unmarried or widowed to remain as they are, considering their present circumstances.

- Paul provides guidance for those who are engaged, advising them on how to handle their relationship in a God-honoring way.

- Paul encourages the Corinthians to exercise their Christian liberty wisely, considering the impact of their actions on others.

What stands out to you in this chapter?

Where do you see God in this chapter?

How have you been challenged while reading this chapter?

Any lingering thoughts or questions following the reading?

Read 1 Corinthians 8   **Date** _____

Recap:

- Paul addresses the issue of food offered to idols, which was a common concern in the Corinthian church.

- Paul acknowledges that "knowledge puffs up" but love edifies.

- He warns against using knowledge as a source of pride, emphasizing the importance of love in interactions with others.

- Paul cautions those with knowledge not to cause the weak believers to stumble by eating food offered to idols.

- Paul emphasizes the importance of considering the impact of our actions on the church community, aiming to build one another up in love.

- Paul warns against causing another believer to stumble or fall away by disregarding their conscience.

What stands out to you in this chapter?

Where do you see God in this chapter?

How have you been challenged while reading this chapter?

Any lingering thoughts or questions following the reading?

ead 1 Corinthians 9   **Date** _____

ecap:

- Paul defends his apostleship and asserts his right as an apostle to eat and drink and have a believing wife, just like the other apostles.

- Paul affirms that he has the right to receive material support from the Corinthians for his ministry, but he has chosen not to exercise this right to avoid hindering the Gospel.

- Paul describes his dedication to preaching the Gospel and his willingness to labor and endure hardships to share the message of Christ.

- Paul explains that he adapts his approach to different groups of people to better connect with them and share the Gospel effectively.

- Paul urges believers to run the race of the Christian life with determination and purpose, aiming for the heavenly prize.

- Paul stresses the importance of discipline and self-control in the Christian life, so he is not disqualified from the race.

What stands out to you in this chapter?

Where do you see God in this chapter?

How have you been challenged while reading this chapter?

Any lingering thoughts or questions following the reading?

Read 1 Corinthians 10   **Date** _____

Recap:

- Paul draws lessons from Israel's experiences in the wilderness, emphasizing the importance of learning from their mistakes and not repeating them.

- Paul explains that all the Israelites ate the same spiritual food and drink from Christ, the spiritual rock that followed them in the wilderness.

- Paul warns against testing the Lord as the Israelites did in the wilderness, leading to their destruction.

- Paul advises believers to flee from idolatry and any participation in the worship of false gods.

What stands out to you in this chapter?

Where do you see God in this chapter?

How have you been challenged while reading this chapter?

Any lingering thoughts or questions following the reading?

Read 1 Corinthians 11   **Date** _____

Recap:

- Paul reminds the Corinthians of the significance of the Lord's Supper as a participation in the body and blood of Christ.
- We are reminded to check our hearts before partaking, to avoid drinking condemnation onto ourselves.

What stands out to you in this chapter?

Where do you see God in this chapter?

How have you been challenged while reading this chapter?

Any lingering thoughts or questions following the reading?

Read 1 Corinthians 12   **Date** _____

Recap:

- Paul teaches on the diversity of spiritual gifts within the Church and the unity of believers as the body of Christ.

- He emphasizes the importance of each member and their unique contribution to the body.

- This serves as a reminder for believers to value and respect one another's gifts and to work together in unity and love for the edification of the Church.

What stands out to you in this chapter?

Where do you see God in this chapter?

How have you been challenged while reading this chapter?

Any lingering thoughts or questions following the reading?

ead 1 Corinthians 13   **Date** _____

ecap:

- Paul begins by emphasizing the supremacy of love over all other spiritual gifts and actions.

- Paul provides a detailed description of what love is, using characteristics like patience, kindness, humility, selflessness, and forgiveness.

- Paul points out that without love, even the most impressive spiritual gifts and actions are meaningless.

- Paul describes love as enduring, always trusting, and hopeful, even in difficult circumstances.

- Paul states that love is eternal and will never pass away, unlike other temporary gifts and abilities.

- Paul explains that our current understanding is limited, but when perfection comes, we will know fully, just as God knows us.

What stands out to you in this chapter?

Where do you see God in this chapter?

How have you been challenged while reading this chapter?

Any lingering thoughts or questions following the reading?

Read 1 Corinthians 14   **Date** _____

Recap:

- Paul encourages the Corinthians to desire the gift of prophecy over speaking in tongues, as prophecy is more beneficial for the edification of the church.

- Paul acknowledges that speaking in tongues can edify the speaker personally but it does not edify the rest of the church unless there is interpretation.

- Paul explains that prophecy, which involves speaking in a known language with understanding, edifies the entire church.

- Paul emphasizes the need for clarity in communication during public worship, so that everyone can understand and be built up.

- Paul instructs that everything in the church should be done in an orderly and respectful manner, avoiding confusion and chaos.

- Paul affirms that speaking in tongues in private prayer is allowed, as it is a form of personal communication with God.

What stands out to you in this chapter?

Where do you see God in this chapter?

How have you been challenged while reading this chapter?

Any lingering thoughts or questions following the reading?

Read 1 Corinthians 15   **Date** _____

Recap:

- Paul emphasizes the crucial significance of Christ's resurrection, as it is the foundation of the Christian faith.
- Paul affirms that Christ's resurrection is a guarantee of the resurrection of believers, who will be raised with imperishable, glorious bodies.
- Paul declares that the power of sin is in the law, but believers have victory over sin through Christ's resurrection.
- Paul emphasizes the power of the Gospel, which brings salvation to those who believe.

What stands out to you in this chapter?

Where do you see God in this chapter?

How have you been challenged while reading this chapter?

Any lingering thoughts or questions following the reading?

Read 1 Corinthians 16   **Date** _____

Recap:

- Paul shares his travel plans and expresses his desire to visit the Corinthians, but he is currently staying in Ephesus until Pentecost.

- Paul hopes to spend some time with the Corinthians, and he encourages them to welcome Apollos if he decides to visit.

- Paul advises the Corinthians to be alert, stand firm in the faith, be strong, and do everything with love.

- Paul sends greetings from various individuals, including Aquila and Priscilla, and he concludes the letter with a final farewell in his own handwriting.

What stands out to you in this chapter?

Where do you see God in this chapter?

How have you been challenged while reading this chapter?

Any lingering thoughts or questions following the reading?

The Book of 2 Corinthians

ead 2 Corinthians 1   **Date** _____

ecap:

- Paul begins by praising God for being the God of all comfort, who comforts us in all our pain and sorrows.

- Believers share in the sufferings of Christ so that they may also share in His comfort.

- God is faithful and can be trusted to deliver them from troubles and challenges.

- Paul writes with sincerity and honesty, not in condemnation but out of love and concern for the Corinthians.

What stands out to you in this chapter?

Where do you see God in this chapter?

How have you been challenged while reading this chapter?

Any lingering thoughts or questions following the reading?

Read 2 Corinthians 2   **Date** _____

Recap:

- Paul's calls for forgiveness, the sincerity and love in his ministry, and the surpassing glory of the new covenant in Christ.

- Paul is expressing his concern for their relationship with God and urges them to respond to His grace.

- Paul's words reflect his passion for the Gospel and his desire to see the Corinthians grow in their faith and understanding of Christ's redemptive work.

What stands out to you in this chapter?

Where do you see God in this chapter?

How have you been challenged while reading this chapter?

Any lingering thoughts or questions following the reading?

ead 2 Corinthians 3   **Date** _____

Recap:

- Paul's teachings on the new covenant, the transformative work of the Spirit, and the freedom and boldness believers have in Christ.
- The Spirit brings life and righteousness.
- Paul's words encourage believers to behold the glory of the Lord with unveiled faces, embracing the transformative power of the Spirit and reflecting Christ's image in their lives.

What stands out to you in this chapter?

Where do you see God in this chapter?

How have you been challenged while reading this chapter?

Any lingering thoughts or questions following the reading?

Read 2 Corinthians 4   **Date** _____

Recap:

- Paul explains that he carries the death of Christ in his body so that the life of Christ may also be revealed in him.

- Paul compares the light of the knowledge of God in Christ to the dawn that shines in the darkness of human hearts.

- The power to endure afflictions and trials comes from God, to show that the surpassing power belongs to Him and not to human abilities.

- Paul reiterates that though he is afflicted, he is not crushed, as the life of Jesus is manifested in his mortal body.

What stands out to you in this chapter?

Where do you see God in this chapter?

How have you been challenged while reading this chapter?

Any lingering thoughts or questions following the reading?

Read 2 Corinthians 5   **Date** _____

Recap:

- Paul encourages believers to walk by faith, not by sight, knowing that their eternal destiny is secured by God.

- Paul emphasizes that believers are now ambassadors for Christ, called to reconcile people to God through the message of reconciliation.

- Paul declares that believers are new creations in Christ, and the old has passed away, giving them a fresh start and a new life.

- Paul urges believers to share the Gospel message with others.

What stands out to you in this chapter?

Where do you see God in this chapter?

How have you been challenged while reading this chapter?

Any lingering thoughts or questions following the reading?

Read 2 Corinthians 6   **Date** _____

Recap:

- Paul shares the trials and challenges he and his fellow workers faced in their ministry, showing their commitment to the Gospel.

- Paul advises believers not to be unequally yoked with unbelievers and to separate themselves from sinful influences.

- Paul exhorts believers to cleanse themselves from all defilement, pursuing holiness and righteousness.

- Paul expresses his love and deep affection for the Corinthians, encouraging them to open their hearts to him.

- Paul acknowledges the hardships and sorrows he faced in his ministry, yet he rejoices in God's comfort and encouragement.

What stands out to you in this chapter?

Where do you see God in this chapter?

How have you been challenged while reading this chapter?

Any lingering thoughts or questions following the reading?

Read 2 Corinthians 7   **Date** _____

Recap:

- Paul expresses his love and concern for the Corinthians, recounting the comfort and encouragement he received from Titus' report about their changed hearts.

- He also commends them for their earnestness in dealing with the issues that arose within the church.

- Paul writes about the godly sorrow that leads to repentance and contrasts it with worldly sorrow that leads to death.

- He rejoices that their sorrow brought about repentance and restoration, resulting in a deeper commitment to God.

- He encourages them to continue their spiritual growth and to maintain a strong relationship with him and other believers.

What stands out to you in this chapter?

Where do you see God in this chapter?

How have you been challenged while reading this chapter?

Any lingering thoughts or questions following the reading?

Read 2 Corinthians 8   **Date** _____

Recap:

- Paul commends the churches in Macedonia for their generosity and willingness to give, even while in poverty.

- The Macedonians gave beyond their means, motivated by God's grace working in their hearts

What stands out to you in this chapter?

Where do you see God in this chapter?

How have you been challenged while reading this chapter?

Any lingering thoughts or questions following the reading?

ead 2 Corinthians 9   **Date** _____

ecap:

- Paul points to the selflessness of Christ, who, though rich, became poor for the sake of believers' salvation, as the ultimate model of giving.
- Paul emphasizes that giving should come from a willing heart, not under compulsion, and that God loves a cheerful giver.

What stands out to you in this chapter?

Where do you see God in this chapter?

How have you been challenged while reading this chapter?

Any lingering thoughts or questions following the reading?

Read 2 Corinthians 10   **Date** _____

Recap:

- Paul's defense of his apostolic authority and the spiritual nature of his warfare.

- The Corinthians need to recognize and submit to the authority that God has given to Paul.

- Paul's words also emphasize his desire for the Corinthians' spiritual maturity and obedience to Christ.

- The Corinthians need to embrace the true source of spiritual authority and discernment as they seek to grow in their faith and build up the body of Christ.

What stands out to you in this chapter?

Where do you see God in this chapter?

How have you been challenged while reading this chapter?

Any lingering thoughts or questions following the reading?

ead 2 Corinthians 11

Date _____

ecap:

- Paul expresses his concern that the Corinthians might be led astray by false apostles who are preaching a different gospel.

- Paul boasts in his weaknesses, as he believes that God's power is made perfect in weakness.

- Paul warns the Corinthians about the danger of being deceived by false apostles who are preaching a different Jesus and a different gospel.

- Paul warns that Satan himself can disguise himself as an angel of light to deceive people.

- Paul denies taking money from the Corinthians, highlighting his desire to avoid any accusation of financial gain.

What stands out to you in this chapter?

Where do you see God in this chapter?

How have you been challenged while reading this chapter?

Any lingering thoughts or questions following the reading?

Read 2 Corinthians 12　　　　　　　　　　　**Date** _____

Recap:

- Paul reveals that he was given a thorn in the flesh, a messenger of Satan, to keep him from becoming conceited because of the surpassing greatness of hi revelations.

- Paul expresses his fear that when he comes to them, he may find them not as he wishes and that there may be strife, jealousy, fits of anger, divisions, and other sins among them.

- Paul urges the Corinthians to examine themselves, to see if they are truly in the faith, and to test whether Christ is in them.

- Paul urges the Corinthians to repent of their sins before he comes, so that he may not have to be harsh when he visits them.

What stands out to you in this chapter?

Where do you see God in this chapter?

How have you been challenged while reading this chapter?

Any lingering thoughts or questions following the reading?

ead 2 Corinthians 13   **Date** _____

ecap:

- Paul reminds the Corinthians that this will be his third visit to them.

- Paul warns that he will not spare any who persist in sin, just as he warned during his second visit.

- Paul declares that Christ is not weak in dealing with them but is powerful among them.

- Paul prays for their restoration to a state of spiritual maturity.

What stands out to you in this chapter?

Where do you see God in this chapter?

How have you been challenged while reading this chapter?

Any lingering thoughts or questions following the reading?

The Book of Exodus

Read Exodus 1   **Date** _____

Recap:
- The Israelites multiplied and became a large nation.
- To control the Israelite population, Pharaoh imposes harsh and oppressive labor upon them. The Israelites are forced into slave labor, building cities and working in harsh conditions.
- Pharaoh orders the Hebrew midwives to kill all male babies born to the Israelites, but the midwives fear God and do not obey the command.
- When Moses' mother can no longer hide him, she places him in a basket made of reeds and sets him adrift on the Nile River, trusting God to protect him.
- Pharaoh's daughter discovers the baby Moses in the basket while bathing in the Nile. She decides to adopt him as her own son.

What stands out to you in this chapter?
Where do you see God in this chapter?
How have you been challenged while reading this chapter?
Any lingering thoughts or questions following the reading?

Read Exodus 2   **Date** _____

Recap:

- Pharaoh's daughter employs Moses' own mother as his nurse, allowing her to care for him and nurse him during his early years.

- Moses grows up in Pharaoh's palace and receives an education and training befitting a prince of Egypt.

- One day, as Moses observes an Egyptian taskmaster beating an Israelite slave, he intervWhen news of the killing reaches Pharaoh, Moses fears for his life and flees from Egypt to the land of Midian.

What stands out to you in this chapter?

Where do you see God in this chapter?

How have you been challenged while reading this chapter?

Any lingering thoughts or questions following the reading?

Read Exodus 3   **Date** _____

Recap:

- The Lord speaks to Moses from the burning bush on Mount Sanai, calling him by name and instructing him to remove his sandals because the ground he is standing on is holy.

- The Lord identifies Himself as the God of Abraham, Isaac, and Jacob, making it clear that He is the same God who made covenants with their ancestors.

- God tells Moses that He has seen the affliction of the Israelites in Egypt and heard their cries because of their oppressors. He expresses His concern for their suffering.

- Moses is hesitant and questions his ability to lead the Israelites and carry out God's plan. He feels unworthy and unqualified for the task.

- God assures Moses that He will be with him and promises to be a constant presence and source of strength.

What stands out to you in this chapter?

Where do you see God in this chapter?

How have you been challenged while reading this chapter?

Any lingering thoughts or questions following the reading?

Read Exodus 4   **Date** _____

Recap:

- God grants Moses three miraculous signs: turning his staff into a serpent, making his hand leprous and then healing it, and turning water from the Nile into blood.

- God reassures Moses by appointing his brother Aaron as his spokesperson, who will convey God's messages to the people and to Pharaoh.

- Moses and Aaron go before Pharaoh to demand the release of the Israelites from slavery. However, Pharaoh remains stubborn and refuses to let them go.

What stands out to you in this chapter?

Where do you see God in this chapter?

How have you been challenged while reading this chapter?

Any lingering thoughts or questions following the reading?

Read Exodus 5   Date _____

Recap:

- Pharaoh responds harshly to Moses and Aaron, refusing to let the Israelites go.

- Pharaoh orders the taskmasters to make the Israelite slaves work harder, requiring them to gather their own straw while still meeting the same quota (bricks.

- Moses questions God, asking why He allowed the situation to worsen for the Israelites.

- God reassures Moses that He will deliver the Israelites from their bondage and fulfill His covenant with them.

- Moses complains again to God, then God reaffirms His promise to deliver the Israelites from Egypt and assures Moses that He will perform mighty acts of judgment against Pharaoh.

What stands out to you in this chapter?

Where do you see God in this chapter?

How have you been challenged while reading this chapter?

Any lingering thoughts or questions following the reading?

ead Exodus 6   **Date** _____

ecap:

- God reminds Moses of the covenant He made with Abraham, Isaac, and Jacob to give them the land of Canaan as their possession.

- God appoints Aaron as Moses' mouthpiece, and Moses is to speak to Aaron, who will relay God's words to Pharaoh and the people.

- Moses and Aaron relay God's message to the Israelite elders, and this time the people listen and believe that God will deliver them.

- Moses expresses doubt about his effectiveness, considering his speech impediment. However, God reaffirms His call and instructs Moses to speak His words fearlessly.

What stands out to you in this chapter?

Where do you see God in this chapter?

How have you been challenged while reading this chapter?

Any lingering thoughts or questions following the reading?

Read Exodus 7   **Date** _____

Recap:

- As a consequence of Pharaoh's hardened heart, God turns the Nile River and all its water into blood, making it undrinkable. (Plague #1)

- God instructs Aaron to stretch his hand over Egypt to bring forth frogs, and the land is plagued with an overwhelming number of frogs. (Plague #2)

- Moses allows Pharaoh to set the time for the removal of the frogs, and when they perish, the land is filled with their stench.

- God commands Aaron to strike the dust of the earth with his staff, and it becomes lice throughout all the land of Egypt.(Plague #3)

- Despite the plagues, Pharaoh remains defiant and refuses to let the Israelites go.

What stands out to you in this chapter?

Where do you see God in this chapter?

How have you been challenged while reading this chapter?

Any lingering thoughts or questions following the reading?

ead Exodus 8   **Date** _____

ecap:

- As a sign of God's power, Aaron casts down his staff before Pharaoh and it becomes a serpent. However, Pharaoh's magicians also replicate the feat with their enchantments.

- Swarms of Flies (Plague #4)

- Despite the plagues, Pharaoh remains defiant and refuses to let the Israelites go.

What stands out to you in this chapter?

Where do you see God in this chapter?

How have you been challenged while reading this chapter?

Any lingering thoughts or questions following the reading?

Read Exodus 9   **Date** _____

Recap:

- All the livestock in the land was killed (Plague #5)

- Boils fell on all the people in the land (Plague #6)

- God sends a severe hailstorm upon Egypt, accompanied by thunder and fire. The hail destroys crops, trees, and animals throughout the land, except in the land of Goshen where the Israelites reside. (Plague #7)

- Pharaoh admits his sin and wrongdoing in refusing to let the Israelites go and pleads with Moses and Aaron to intercede with God to stop the hail.

- Moses' prayer and the end of the hail: Moses prays to God, and the hailstorm ceases. However, Pharaoh's heart remains hardened, and he still does not release the Israelites.

What stands out to you in this chapter?

Where do you see God in this chapter?

How have you been challenged while reading this chapter?

Any lingering thoughts or questions following the reading?

Read Exodus 10   **Date** _____

Recap:

- God sends a plague of locusts upon Egypt, covering the land and devouring what little vegetation remained after the hail.(Plague #8)

- God sends darkness upon Egypt, covering the land in a thick darkness that lasts for three days. The darkness is so intense that it can be felt. (Plague #9)

- Moses warned Pharaoh of the impending tenth and final plague—the death of the firstborn in all the land of Egypt, including Pharaoh's own house.

- God instructs the Israelites to take a lamb, sacrifice it, and mark their doorposts with its blood, so the angel of death will pass over their homes during the final plague.

What stands out to you in this chapter?

Where do you see God in this chapter?

How have you been challenged while reading this chapter?

Any lingering thoughts or questions following the reading?

Read Exodus 11   **Date** _____

Recap:

- Moses warned Pharaoh of the impending tenth and final plague—the death of the firstborn in all the land of Egypt, including Pharaoh's own house.
- Pharaoh's heart was still hard.

What stands out to you in this chapter?

Where do you see God in this chapter?

How have you been challenged while reading this chapter?

Any lingering thoughts or questions following the reading?

ead Exodus 12   **Date** _____

ecap:

- God instructs the Israelites to take a lamb, sacrifice it, and mark their doorposts with its blood, so the angel of death will pass over their homes during the final plague.

- The Israelites are instructed to roast the lamb and eat it with unleavened bread and bitter herbs. They are to eat it in haste, with their belts fastened, sandals on their feet, and staff in hand, ready to leave Egypt.

- At midnight, the Lord strikes down all the firstborn in the land of Egypt, from Pharaoh's firstborn to the prisoners in the dungeon and even the firstborn of the livestock.

- A great cry arises in Egypt due to the death of the firstborn, and Pharaoh finally relents and summons Moses and Aaron to leave Egypt along with all the Israelites.

- God instructs the Israelites to observe the Feast of Unleavened Bread, a seven-day feast during which they are to eat unleavened bread and remove all leaven from their homes.

- The Passover serves as a reminder of God's deliverance and redemption of the Israelites from slavery in Egypt. It becomes a crucial event in the history of Israel and is commemorated annually as a symbol of God's faithfulness.

What stands out to you in this chapter?

Where do you see God in this chapter?

How have you been challenged while reading this chapter?

Any lingering thoughts or questions following the reading?

Read Exodus 13   **Date** _____

Recap:

- Moses tells the Israelites that when they come into the land of Canaan, they are to dedicate every firstborn male to God or redeem the firstborn donkey with a lamb.

- Instead of taking the shorter route through the Philistine country, God leads the Israelites toward the Red Sea, fearing that the people might change their minds if they face war.

- When Pharaoh learns that the Israelites are trapped between the wilderness and the sea, he regrets letting them go and pursues them with his army.

What stands out to you in this chapter?

Where do you see God in this chapter?

How have you been challenged while reading this chapter?

Any lingering thoughts or questions following the reading?

Read Exodus 14   **Date** _____

Recap:

- God miraculously parts the Red Sea, allowing the Israelites to pass through on dry ground, and then brings the waters back to drown the Egyptian army.

- Miriam, the sister of Moses and Aaron, leads the women in a song of praise and thanksgiving to God for the miraculous deliverance at the Red Sea.

- The Egyptians follow the Israelites into the parted sea but face confusion as their chariot wheels get stuck.

- As the Israelites reach the other side, Moses stretches out his hand again, and the waters return to their place, drowning the entire Egyptian army.

What stands out to you in this chapter?

Where do you see God in this chapter?

How have you been challenged while reading this chapter?

Any lingering thoughts or questions following the reading?

Read Exodus 15   **Date** _____

Recap:

- After the miraculous crossing of the Red Sea and the drowning of the Egyptian army, Moses and the Israelites sing a triumphant song of praise and thanksgiving to God for His deliverance.

- Miriam leads the women in dancing and singing, praising God for His wondrous deeds and His deliverance of the Israelites.

- The Israelites journey from Marah to Elim, where they find twelve springs and seventy palm trees, providing them with water and shade.

What stands out to you in this chapter?

Where do you see God in this chapter?

How have you been challenged while reading this chapter?

Any lingering thoughts or questions following the reading?

ead Exodus 16   **Date** _____

ecap:

- The Israelites travel from Elim to the wilderness of Sin and complain about the lack of food, expressing their desire to have died in Egypt where they had plenty to eat.

- God hears the people's complaints and provides them with manna, a bread-like substance that appears on the ground every morning, sustaining them throughout their journey.

- God instructs the Israelites to gather twice as much manna on the sixth day to observe the Sabbath, a day of rest, during which no manna will appear.

- God tests the people's obedience to His commandments and their faithfulness in keeping His instructions regarding the gathering of manna.

What stands out to you in this chapter?

Where do you see God in this chapter?

How have you been challenged while reading this chapter?

Any lingering thoughts or questions following the reading?

Read Exodus 17   **Date** _____

Recap:

- The Israelites journey from the wilderness of Sin to Rephidim but find no water to drink, leading them to complain against Moses and question God's presence among them.

- God tells Moses to take his staff and strike the rock at Horeb (Mount Sinai), and water will come out for the people to drink.

- Moses does as God commands, striking the rock, and water gushes forth, providing enough for all the people and their livestock.

- The Amalekites attack the Israelites at Rephidim, prompting Moses to choose Joshua to lead the Israelite army into battle.

- God tells Moses to write in a book as a memorial that He will utterly blot out the remembrance of Amalek from under heaven.

What stands out to you in this chapter?

Where do you see God in this chapter?

How have you been challenged while reading this chapter?

Any lingering thoughts or questions following the reading?

Read Exodus 18   **Date** _____

Recap:

- Moses tells Jethro about all the miraculous deliverance from Egypt, the parting of the Red Sea, and God's provision and guidance in the wilderness.

- Jethro observes Moses judging the people from morning till evening and advises him to appoint capable leaders to help shoulder the burden of judging and resolving disputes among the people.

- Moses follows Jethro's advice and appoints capable and trustworthy men to serve as rulers over thousands, hundreds, fifties, and tens to judge the people.

What stands out to you in this chapter?

Where do you see God in this chapter?

How have you been challenged while reading this chapter?

Any lingering thoughts or questions following the reading?

Read Exodus 19   **Date** _____

Recap:

- God calls Moses to come up to the mountain, and He instructs Moses to remind the people of all that He has done for them in bringing them out of Egypt.

- God tells Moses that if the Israelites obey His voice and keep His covenant, they will be a treasured possession, a kingdom of priests, and a holy nation.

- God establishes boundaries around the mountain, warning the people not to touch it or approach it, lest they die.

- On the third day, there is thunder, lightning, a thick cloud, and the sound of a trumpet as God comes down on Mount Sinai in fire, and the mountain is covered in smoke.

What stands out to you in this chapter?

Where do you see God in this chapter?

How have you been challenged while reading this chapter?

Any lingering thoughts or questions following the reading?

Read Exodus 20   **Date** _____

Recap:

- The Lord speaks the Ten Commandments to the people from the midst of the fire and the cloud.
- The people tremble with fear at the awesome display of God's presence and ask Moses to speak to them on God's behalf because they are afraid they will die if God continues to speak to them directly.

What stands out to you in this chapter?

Where do you see God in this chapter?

How have you been challenged while reading this chapter?

Any lingering thoughts or questions following the reading?

Read Exodus 21   **Date** _____

Recap:

- God provides regulations concerning the treatment of Hebrew slaves, ensuring their fair treatment and granting them freedom after six years of service.

- If a Hebrew slave loves their master and wishes to stay, they can voluntarily choose to become a lifelong servant.

- God establishes laws for the treatment of female slaves, guaranteeing their rights and dignity.

- Laws about the consequences and compensation for various personal injuries, including those caused by oxen, pits, or other dangerous circumstances.

- The principle of "an eye for an eye, a tooth for a tooth" is introduced, indicating that the punishment should match the injury inflicted in cases of personal harm.

- If someone's animal causes injury or death to another person, the owner is held responsible, and appropriate compensation is required.

What stands out to you in this chapter?

Where do you see God in this chapter?

How have you been challenged while reading this chapter?

Any lingering thoughts or questions following the reading?

Read Exodus 22   **Date** _____

Recap:

- Laws about restitution for theft are established, with thieves required to repay double the value of what they stole.

- Laws about property damage and the appropriate compensation for damages are outlined, along with Laws about Seduction, Capital offenses, Protecting the Vulnerable, and having respect for God.

What stands out to you in this chapter?

Where do you see God in this chapter?

How have you been challenged while reading this chapter?

Any lingering thoughts or questions following the reading?

Read Exodus 23   **Date** _____

Recap:

- God instructs the Israelites not to spread false reports, participate in wickedness, or side with a crowd to pervert justice.

- They are to be impartial in legal disputes and not favor the poor or the powerful.

- God emphasizes the importance of observing the Sabbath, a day of rest, for both the people and their animals.

What stands out to you in this chapter?

Where do you see God in this chapter?

How have you been challenged while reading this chapter?

Any lingering thoughts or questions following the reading?

Read Exodus 24

Date _____

Recap:

- God instructs Moses, along with Aaron, Nadab, Abihu, and seventy elders of Israel, to come up the mountain to worship Him from a distance.
- After the vision of God, they have a covenant meal together, a symbol of the close relationship between God and the leaders of Israel.
- Moses remains on the mountain for forty days and forty nights in communion with God.

What stands out to you in this chapter?

Where do you see God in this chapter?

How have you been challenged while reading this chapter?

Any lingering thoughts or questions following the reading?

Read Exodus 25   **Date** _____

Recap:

- God instructs Moses to tell the Israelites to bring offerings willingly, includin gold, silver, bronze, fine linen, and various materials for the construction of the tabernacle.

- God provides detailed instructions for building the Ark of the Covenant, a sacred chest that will house the stone tablets with the Ten Commandments.

- God instructs the construction of the Mercy Seat, a cover for the Ark made of pure gold with two cherubim facing each other, where God will meet with Moses and speak to him.

- God provides instructions for constructing a table of acacia wood overlaid with gold, on which the Bread of the Presence will be placed before Him continually.

- God instructs the making of a seven-branched lampstand of pure gold, with its lamps and tongs, to provide light in the tabernacle.

What stands out to you in this chapter?

Where do you see God in this chapter?

How have you been challenged while reading this chapter?

Any lingering thoughts or questions following the reading?

Read Exodus 26   **Date** _____

Recap:

- God provides specifications for the length, width, and height of the Tabernacle, which is to be made of boards of acacia wood covered with gold.

- God commands the making of a veil of blue, purple, and scarlet yarn and fine linen, with cherubim woven into it, to separate the Holy Place from the Most Holy Place.

- God reminds Moses of the Ark of the Testimony, or the Ark of the Covenant, which is to be placed in the Most Holy Place within the Tabernacle.

- The Tabernacle serves as a place for God to dwell among the Israelites, and it is to be set up according to the pattern shown to Moses on the mountain.

What stands out to you in this chapter?

Where do you see God in this chapter?

How have you been challenged while reading this chapter?

Any lingering thoughts or questions following the reading?

Read Exodus 27   **Date** _____

Recap:

- God provides detailed instructions for constructing the Altar of Burnt Offering, which is to be made of acacia wood overlaid with bronze and located in the courtyard of the Tabernacle.

- God gives instructions for the courtyard surrounding the Tabernacle, providing details on its size, the materials used for its curtains, and the pillars holding them in place.

- God instructs the Israelites to bring clear oil made from crushed olives for the lamp that will burn continually in the Tabernacle.

What stands out to you in this chapter?

Where do you see God in this chapter?

How have you been challenged while reading this chapter?

Any lingering thoughts or questions following the reading?

Read Exodus 28   **Date** _____

Recap:

- God instructs the making of special garments for Aaron and his sons to wear while serving in the Tabernacle.
- God commands the making of the breastpiece, which is to be adorned with twelve gemstones representing the twelve tribes of Israel.
- God instructs the making of the robe of the ephod and the turban for Aaron, with a gold plate engraved with the words "Holy to the Lord."

What stands out to you in this chapter?

Where do you see God in this chapter?

How have you been challenged while reading this chapter?

Any lingering thoughts or questions following the reading?

Read Exodus 29   **Date** _____

Recap:

- God instructs Moses to anoint Aaron and his sons with the special anointing oil and consecrate them for the priesthood.

- The priesthood is to be a perpetual statute for Aaron and his descendants afte him.

- The garments and consecration of the priests symbolize God's presence and holiness among the Israelites and their approach to Him through designated representatives.

- Aaron and his sons are to offer a young bull as a sin offering to atone for thei sins and purify themselves before serving as priests.

- A ram is to be offered as a burnt offering, symbolizing their dedication and commitment to serving God.

What stands out to you in this chapter?

Where do you see God in this chapter?

How have you been challenged while reading this chapter?

Any lingering thoughts or questions following the reading?

ead Exodus 30   **Date** _____

ecap:

- God provides a specific formula for making the sacred incense to be burned on the Altar of Incense, which is not to be used for any other purpose.

- God commands a census to be taken of the Israelites and requires that each person, regardless of their status, give a half-shekel of silver as an offering for the service of the Tabernacle.

- God instructs the making of a bronze basin and its stand, which will be used for the priests to wash their hands and feet before entering the Tabernacle.

- God gives the recipe for making the anointing oil, which is used to consecrate the priests and the sacred items in the Tabernacle, and the sacred incense, which is not to be made for personal use.

What stands out to you in this chapter?

Where do you see God in this chapter?

How have you been challenged while reading this chapter?

Any lingering thoughts or questions following the reading?

Read Exodus 31   **Date** _____

Recap:

- God reiterates the importance of observing the Sabbath day as a day of rest and holy restfulness, and it is to be kept as a perpetual covenant throughout the generations.

- God's emphasis on the observance of the Sabbath as a perpetual covenant demonstrates the enduring significance of rest and worship in the Israelites

What stands out to you in this chapter?

Where do you see God in this chapter?

How have you been challenged while reading this chapter?

Any lingering thoughts or questions following the reading?

ead Exodus 32   **Date** _____

ecap:

- While Moses is on Mount Sinai receiving the instructions from God, the people become impatient and ask Aaron to make them a god to worship.

- Aaron complies and makes a golden calf for the people to worship.

- The people worship the golden calf as a representation of God and engage in revelry and immoral behavior, breaking the commandment against idolatry and disobeying God's law.

- God becomes angry with the people and plans to destroy them, but Moses intercedes on their behalf, asking God to relent from His wrath and remember His covenant with Abraham, Isaac, and Jacob.

- Moses burns the golden calf, grinds it into powder, scatters it in the water, and makes the Israelites drink it as a punishment for their sin.

- God tells Moses that only those who have sinned against Him will be blotted out of His book, and He assures Moses that He will lead the people as promised.

What stands out to you in this chapter?

Where do you see God in this chapter?

How have you been challenged while reading this chapter?

Any lingering thoughts or questions following the reading?

Read Exodus 33   **Date** _____

Recap:

- Moses sets up the Tent of Meeting outside the camp, and everyone who seek the Lord goes to the tent.

- The Lord speaks to Moses face to face, as a man speaks to his friend, inside the Tent of Meeting.

- God proclaims His name to Moses, emphasizing His mercy, compassion, an forgiveness.

What stands out to you in this chapter?

Where do you see God in this chapter?

How have you been challenged while reading this chapter?

Any lingering thoughts or questions following the reading?

.ead Exodus 34   **Date** _____

ecap:

- God commands Moses to cut two new tablets of stone like the first ones, as the first tablets were shattered when Moses saw the worship of the Golden Calf.

- Moses quickly bows down and worships the Lord and asks for God's favor, acknowledging the sinful state of the people and pleading for forgiveness and acceptance.

- God reaffirms the covenant with the Israelites, promising to perform wonders and drive out the inhabitants of the land before them.

What stands out to you in this chapter?

Where do you see God in this chapter?

How have you been challenged while reading this chapter?

Any lingering thoughts or questions following the reading?

Read Exodus 35   **Date** _____

Recap:

- Moses gathers the Israelites and reminds them of the importance of observing the Sabbath as a day of rest and holy restfulness.

- Moses instructs the people to take from among them a contribution for the Lord to build the Tabernacle and its furnishings.

- The Israelites respond generously and with willing hearts, bringing various offerings of gold, silver, bronze, fine linen, and other materials for the construction of the Tabernacle.

What stands out to you in this chapter?

Where do you see God in this chapter?

How have you been challenged while reading this chapter?

Any lingering thoughts or questions following the reading?

Read Exodus 36   **Date** _____

Recap:

- Bezalel, Oholiab, and others, who were filled with the Spirit of God, begin the construction of the Tabernacle and its furnishings.

- The Ark is made with acacia wood, overlaid with gold, and its carrying poles are inserted into its rings.

- The Basin, made of bronze with a base made from bronze mirrors, is skillfully crafted for the priests to wash their hands and feet.

- As the Tabernacle is assembled, the glory of the Lord fills the Tabernacle, indicating His approval and presence.

What stands out to you in this chapter?

Where do you see God in this chapter?

How have you been challenged while reading this chapter?

Any lingering thoughts or questions following the reading?

Read Exodus 37   **Date** _____

Recap:

- The Ark's cover, known as the Mercy Seat, is made with pure gold, with two cherubim facing each other.
- Bezalel makes the Table with acacia wood, overlaid with pure gold, and add a gold molding around it.
- The Lampstand is made of pure gold, including its base and flower-like cups.
- Bezalel prepares the sacred anointing oil and the fragrant incense, following God's specific instructions.

What stands out to you in this chapter?

Where do you see God in this chapter?

How have you been challenged while reading this chapter?

Any lingering thoughts or questions following the reading?

Read Exodus 38   **Date** _____

Recap:

- Bezalel makes the Altar of acacia wood, overlaid with bronze, and constructs its bronze grating, carrying poles, and utensils.

- Bezalel makes the Basin and its stand from bronze mirrors donated by the women who served at the entrance of the Tent of Meeting.

- The courtyard is constructed with curtains made of fine linen, supported by bronze pillars with silver hooks and bands.

- All the elements of the Tabernacle, including the Tent of Meeting, the Ark of the Covenant, the Altar of Burnt Offering, and the Basin, are completed according to God's instructions.

What stands out to you in this chapter?

Where do you see God in this chapter?

How have you been challenged while reading this chapter?

Any lingering thoughts or questions following the reading?

Read Exodus 39   **Date** _____

Recap:

- The skilled craftsmen, under the leadership of Bezalel, make the sacred garments for Aaron the high priest, including the ephod, breastpiece, robe, tunics, turban, and sashes, all as God commanded.

- The ephod is made of gold, blue, purple, and scarlet yarn, and fine linen, with two shoulder pieces joined by onyx stones engraved with the names of the twelve tribes of Israel.

- The breastpiece is made with gold, blue, purple, and scarlet yarn, and fine linen, with twelve precious stones representing the twelve tribes of Israel.

- The robe is made entirely of blue, with an opening for the head, and bells of gold and pomegranates of blue, purple, and scarlet yarn are attached to its hem, as God commanded.

- Moses inspects all the work done by the craftsmen and sees that everything is done according to God's instructions. He blesses them for their skill and obedience.

What stands out to you in this chapter?

Where do you see God in this chapter?

How have you been challenged while reading this chapter?

Any lingering thoughts or questions following the reading?

ead Exodus 40   **Date** _____

ecap:

- God instructs Moses to set up the Tabernacle on the first day of the first month, following a year since the Israelites left Egypt.

- Moses puts the Testimony (the two tablets of the Ten Commandments) into the Ark and puts the poles in place for carrying it.

- Moses arranges the Lampstand with its lamps and the Table for the Bread of the Presence on the north side of the Tabernacle.

- Moses places the Altar of Burnt Offering and the Bronze Basin between the Tent of Meeting and the Altar.

- As the Tabernacle is completed and consecrated, the cloud of God's glory covers it, signifying His presence among His people.

What stands out to you in this chapter?

Where do you see God in this chapter?

How have you been challenged while reading this chapter?

Any lingering thoughts or questions following the reading?

The Book of James

Read James 1   **Date** _____

Recap:

- We are to consider our trials and find the "joy" in them.

- James distinguishes between temptation and testing, emphasizing that God does not tempt anyone to do evil.

- He is teaching that every good and perfect gift comes from God, emphasizin His unchanging nature and role as the Father.

What stands out to you in this chapter?

Where do you see God in this chapter?

How have you been challenged while reading this chapter?

Any lingering thoughts or questions following the reading?

ead James 2   **Date** _____

ecap:

- He emphasizes that true faith in Christ should be evident through actions and good works, not merely through empty words or beliefs.

- James stresses the importance of showing mercy and love to others, as God will judge without mercy those who have shown no mercy.

- James concludes that faith without works is dead, and genuine faith will always produce fruit in the form of righteous deeds.

What stands out to you in this chapter?

Where do you see God in this chapter?

How have you been challenged while reading this chapter?

Any lingering thoughts or questions following the reading?

Read James 3   **Date** _____

Recap:

- James begins by warning about the power and potential destructiveness of th tongue, comparing it to a small spark that can ignite a great fire.

- James highlights the fruits of godly wisdom, including good conduct and a willingness to make peace, rather than fostering division or strife.

- He advises against harboring bitter jealousy and selfish ambition, which are often the root causes of conflicts and quarrels.

What stands out to you in this chapter?

Where do you see God in this chapter?

How have you been challenged while reading this chapter?

Any lingering thoughts or questions following the reading?

Read James 4   **Date** _____

Recap:

- He encourages readers to submit to God, resist the temptations of pride, and draw near to Him through repentance and humility.

- James emphasizes that God opposes the proud but gives grace to the humble, urging believers to humble themselves before the Lord.

- He cautions against slander and gossip, urging Christians to respect one another and speak with kindness and love.

- James concludes that failing to do what is right, especially when we know better, is sinful, highlighting the significance of aligning our lives with God's purposes.

What stands out to you in this chapter?

Where do you see God in this chapter?

How have you been challenged while reading this chapter?

Any lingering thoughts or questions following the reading?

Read James 5   **Date** _____

Recap:

- James opens with a great warning to the rich.

- Believers are to remain patient while they await the Lord's return.

- Lay hands on those who are sick and pray for them.

What stands out to you in this chapter?

Where do you see God in this chapter?

How have you been challenged while reading this chapter?

Any lingering thoughts or questions following the reading?

The Book of Judges

Read Judges 1   **Date** _____

Recap:

- After the death of Joshua, the tribe of Judah is the first to go up and fight against the Canaanites, and God gives them victory over the inhabitants of the land.

- The Canaanites continue to live among the Israelites and become a thorn in their side, oppressing and troubling them.

- The house of Joseph (the tribes of Manasseh and Ephraim) captures the city of Bethel.

- The Canaanites persist in their resistance against the Israelites, living among them and maintaining a presence in the land.

What stands out to you in this chapter?

Where do you see God in this chapter?

How have you been challenged while reading this chapter?

Any lingering thoughts or questions following the reading?

Read Judges 2   **Date** _____

Recap:

- After Joshua's death, a new generation arose that did not personally witness the great deeds of the Lord, including the conquest of the land.

- The new generation of Israelites turns away from the Lord, forsakes His commandments, and follows after other gods, particularly the gods of the Canaanites.

- God becomes angry with the Israelites because of their disobedience and idolatry, breaking the covenant He made with their ancestors.

- Despite the unfaithfulness of the people, God raises up judges to deliver them from their oppressors and lead them back to Him.

- The Angel of the Lord appears to the Israelites to rebuke them for their disobedience and to remind them of God's covenant with their ancestors.

- Some of the people listen to the rebuke and weep, while others continue sinning.

What stands out to you in this chapter?

Where do you see God in this chapter?

How have you been challenged while reading this chapter?

Any lingering thoughts or questions following the reading?

ead Judges 3   **Date** _____

ecap:

- The Israelites intermarry with the Canaanites, follow their gods, and forsake the Lord, breaking His commandments.

- God raises up Othniel, the son of Caleb's younger brother Kenaz, as the first judge to deliver the Israelites from Cushan-Rishathaim's oppression.

- God raises up Ehud, a left-handed man from the tribe of Benjamin, to deliver the Israelites from Eglon's oppression.

- Ehud presents a tribute to Eglon but then surprises him by assassinating him with a hidden sword and Ehud escapes.

What stands out to you in this chapter?

Where do you see God in this chapter?

How have you been challenged while reading this chapter?

Any lingering thoughts or questions following the reading?

Read Judges 4   **Date** _____

Recap:

- God raises up Deborah, a prophetess, and Barak, a military leader, to delive the Israelites from Jabin and Sisera's oppression.

- Deborah and Barak lead the Israelite army to victory over Sisera's forces, wit God's intervention causing confusion and defeat for the Canaanites.

What stands out to you in this chapter?

Where do you see God in this chapter?

How have you been challenged while reading this chapter?

Any lingering thoughts or questions following the reading?

ead Judges 5   **Date** _____

ecap:

- Deborah's song begins with a call to praise the Lord for the victory and deliverance He has brought to the Israelites.

- Deborah, a prophetess and judge, is praised for her role in leading the Israelites and encouraging them to take action against their oppressors.

- Various tribes are praised for their willingness to join the battle and fight for the cause of the Lord.

- The song celebrates the volunteers who willingly offered themselves to serve in the army of the Lord.

- The song concludes with a declaration of the Lord's triumph over His enemies and the establishment of peace and prosperity in the land.

What stands out to you in this chapter?

Where do you see God in this chapter?

How have you been challenged while reading this chapter?

Any lingering thoughts or questions following the reading?

Read Judges 6   **Date** _____

Recap:

- The Israelites again do evil in the sight of the Lord, and God allows the Midianites, along with the Amalekites and other eastern nations, to oppress them.

- The Midianites and their allies invade the land during the time of harvest, destroying the crops and leaving the Israelites impoverished and hungry.

- The Angel of the Lord appears to Gideon while he is threshing wheat in a winepress, hiding from the Midianites.

- Gideon asks for a sign to confirm that the Lord has truly called him. He places a fleece of wool on the ground and asks that the fleece be wet with dew while the ground remains dry.

- Gideon asks for another sign and reverses the request, asking that the fleece be dry while the ground is wet with dew, and the Lord grants his request.

What stands out to you in this chapter?

Where do you see God in this chapter?

How have you been challenged while reading this chapter?

Any lingering thoughts or questions following the reading?

ead Judges 7   **Date** _____

ecap:

- Gideon's army, initially consisting of over 32,000 men, is reduced to only three hundred men by the Lord, to demonstrate that the victory will come through God's power, not human strength.

- The Lord instructs Gideon to choose the men for battle based on their response to the way they drink water from the river.

- Those who lap water like dogs are chosen, while those who kneel down to drink are sent home.

- The Lord encourages Gideon by allowing him to overhear a dream and its interpretation in the camp of the Midianites, indicating that their defeat is certain.

- Gideon and his three hundred men worship the Lord and are equipped with trumpets, empty jars, and torches for the battle.

- At the sound of the trumpet blasts and the breaking of the jars, the three hundred men shout, "A sword for the Lord and for Gideon!" The Midianites are thrown into confusion and chaos, turning on each other in the dark.

What stands out to you in this chapter?

Where do you see God in this chapter?

How have you been challenged while reading this chapter?

Any lingering thoughts or questions following the reading?

Read Judges 8   **Date** _____

Recap:

- After the victory over the Midianites, Gideon and his three hundred men pursue the two remaining Midianite kings, Zebah and Zalmunna.

- Gideon captures the two Midianite kings and punishes the elders of Succoth and Penuel for their refusal to help.

- Gideon personally kills the Midianite kings, avenging the deaths of his brothers who were killed by them.

- Gideon makes an ephod out of the gold, and the ephod becomes a snare for Gideon and his family, leading the people to worship it instead of the Lord.

- The land rested for forty years during the days of Gideon.

- After his successful leadership, Gideon dies and is buried in the tomb of his father Joash in Ophrah.

What stands out to you in this chapter?

Where do you see God in this chapter?

How have you been challenged while reading this chapter?

Any lingering thoughts or questions following the reading?

.ead Judges 9   **Date** _____

.ecap:

- • After the death of Gideon, his son Abimelech seeks to become ruler over Israel. He convinces the leaders of Shechem to support him in his quest for power.

- • Abimelech conspires with his supporters to kill all of his brothers, except for Jotham, who escapes.

- • Jotham, the youngest son of Gideon, delivers a parable to the people of Shechem, denouncing their support for Abimelech and predicting disaster.

- • Abimelech defeats Gaal and his followers, driving them out of Shechem.

- • Rather than be killed by a woman, Abimelech commands his armor-bearer to kill him, to avoid humiliation.

- • After the death of Abimelech, Tola and Jair served as judges over Israel for twenty-three years.

What stands out to you in this chapter?

Where do you see God in this chapter?

How have you been challenged while reading this chapter?

Any lingering thoughts or questions following the reading?

Read Judges 10   **Date** _____

Recap:

- The Israelites cry out to the Lord, confessing their sins and seeking His deliverance.

- God responds to the Israelites' cry, reminding them of their past disobedience and worship of false gods.

- He refuses to help them in their distress.

- The people put away their foreign gods and serve the Lord, demonstrating genuine repentance.

What stands out to you in this chapter?

Where do you see God in this chapter?

How have you been challenged while reading this chapter?

Any lingering thoughts or questions following the reading?

ead Judges 11   **Date** _____

ecap:

- Jephthah agrees to lead the Israelites if they promise to make him their leader if he is victorious over the Ammonites.

- Jephthah reminds the king of Ammon of Israel's rightful possession of the land, dating back to their exodus from Egypt and God's defeat of other nations.

- Jephthah makes a vow to the Lord, promising to offer as a burnt offering whatever comes out of his house to meet him if he returns victorious.

- Jephthah's only daughter comes out to meet him with timbrels and dances, and he is devastated by his vow but fulfills it.

What stands out to you in this chapter?

Where do you see God in this chapter?

How have you been challenged while reading this chapter?

Any lingering thoughts or questions following the reading?

Read Judges 12   **Date** _____

Recap:

- After Jephthah's victory over the Ammonites, the men of Ephraim are offended that they were not called to fight in the battle and confront Jephthah.

- The men of Gilead (Jephthah's tribe) and the men of Ephraim engage in a battle. The Gileadites defeat the Ephraimites and secure control of the Jordan River crossings.

- As the Ephraimites attempt to flee across the Jordan, the Gileadites seize the fords and capture anyone attempting to escape.

- They tested them by asking them to say "Shibboleth," and those who couldn't pronounce it correctly were killed.

- After leading Israel for six years, Jephthah dies and is buried in his city of Gilead.

What stands out to you in this chapter?

Where do you see God in this chapter?

How have you been challenged while reading this chapter?

Any lingering thoughts or questions following the reading?

ead Judges 13   **Date** _____

ecap:

- An angel of the Lord appears to the wife of Manoah, a woman who was previously barren, and tells her that she will conceive and bear a son.
- The woman gives birth to a son named Samson, and he grows and is blessed by the Lord.
- The Spirit of the Lord begins to move Samson in Mahaneh Dan, indicating the beginning of his divine calling.

What stands out to you in this chapter?

Where do you see God in this chapter?

How have you been challenged while reading this chapter?

Any lingering thoughts or questions following the reading?

Read Judges 14   **Date** _____

Recap:

- Samson's parents are troubled by his choice of a Philistine wife and inquire i there is no suitable woman among his own people.

- Samson insists on marrying the Philistine woman, saying, "She is right in my eyes."

- Samson goes to Timnah for his wedding, and during the celebration, he poses a riddle to the Philistine guests, challenging them to solve it.

- Samson's wife reveals the answer to the riddle to the Philistine guests.

- Samson, feeling betrayed, leaves his wife and returns to his parents' house.

What stands out to you in this chapter?

Where do you see God in this chapter?

How have you been challenged while reading this chapter?

Any lingering thoughts or questions following the reading?

ead Judges 15   **Date** _____

ecap:

- After some time, Samson decides to visit his wife in Timnah with a young goat as a gift for reconciliation.

- Samson's father-in-law refuses to allow him to see his wife, suggesting that he now regards her as being given to another man.

- Samson is angry about the situation and catches three hundred foxes.

- He ties their tails together in pairs, sets them on fire with torches, and releases them into the Philistine's standing grain, vineyards, and olive groves, causing massive destruction.

- The Philistines discover that Samson is responsible for the destruction and find out that it was in response to his father-in-law giving Samson's wife to another man. In their anger, they burn her and her father to death.

- In retaliation for his wife's death, Samson strikes the Philistines demonstrating his strength and determination.

What stands out to you in this chapter?

Where do you see God in this chapter?

How have you been challenged while reading this chapter?

Any lingering thoughts or questions following the reading?

Read Judges 16   **Date** _____

Recap:

- Samson falls in love with Delilah, a woman from the Valley of Sorek, who is bribed by the Philistine rulers to find out the secret of his strength.

- Samson finally tells Delilah the true secret of his strength, that his hair has never been cut because he is a Nazirite dedicated to God.

- While Samson sleeps, Delilah cuts off his hair, and the Philistines capture him.

- The Philistines blind Samson and put him to work grinding grain in prison.

- The Lord grants Samson strength, and he pushes against the pillars of the temple, causing it to collapse, killing many Philistines, including the rulers, and himself.

- Samson dies along with the Philistines, and his family comes to recover his body.

What stands out to you in this chapter?

Where do you see God in this chapter?

How have you been challenged while reading this chapter?

Any lingering thoughts or questions following the reading?

.ead Judges 17   **Date** _____

.ecap:

- A man named Micah confesses to his mother that he had stolen eleven hundred shekels of silver from her.

- Micah returns the stolen silver to his mother, who then dedicates it to the Lord to make a carved image and a molded image.

- Micah invites the Levite to stay with him and serve as his priest, offering him food, clothing, and ten shekels of silver per year.

- The Danites pass by Micah's house and recognize the Levite's voice. They inquire of him, asking for God's approval and direction for their journey.

What stands out to you in this chapter?

Where do you see God in this chapter?

How have you been challenged while reading this chapter?

Any lingering thoughts or questions following the reading?

Read Judges 18   **Date** _____

Recap:

- The Danites, having no territory of their own, send five brave men from their clans to explore the land and find a place to settle.

- The Levite encourages the Danites, assuring them that their journey will be prosperous because the Lord is with them.

- Six hundred Danite men set out for Laish, armed for war.

- Micah and his neighbors pursue the Danites, but the Danites threaten them, and Micah is forced to abandon his pursuit of the stolen idols.

- The Danites set up the stolen idols from Micah's house in Dan and institute idolatrous worship.

- The Danites continue to practice idolatry in their new territory, far from the proper worship of the Lord.

What stands out to you in this chapter?

Where do you see God in this chapter?

How have you been challenged while reading this chapter?

Any lingering thoughts or questions following the reading?

ead Judges 19   **Date** _____

ecap:

- A Levite and his concubine traveling through the hill country of Ephraim.

- The Levite discovers the lifeless body of his concubine and takes her home. He then dismembers her body and sends parts of it to all the tribes of Israel as evidence of the wickedness in Gibeah.

- The tribes of Israel send messengers to the people of Benjamin, demanding that the perpetrators of the evil act in Gibeah be handed over for punishment.

- The people of Benjamin, instead of complying with the demand for justice, rally together to defend the men of Gibeah.

What stands out to you in this chapter?

Where do you see God in this chapter?

How have you been challenged while reading this chapter?

Any lingering thoughts or questions following the reading?

Read Judges 20   **Date** _____

Recap:

- The tribes of Israel decide to take action against the tribe of Benjamin for the refusal to hand over the perpetrators of the evil act.

- The tribe of Benjamin refuses to comply with the demand for justice, choosing instead to defend the men of Gibeah.

- Despite the initial defeat, the tribes of Israel regroup and seek guidance from the Lord at Bethel. They fast, offer sacrifices, and inquire of God.

- The Lord promises that Israel will be victorious in battle against Benjamin.

What stands out to you in this chapter?

Where do you see God in this chapter?

How have you been challenged while reading this chapter?

Any lingering thoughts or questions following the reading?

ead Judges 21   **Date** _____

Recap:

- The tribes of Israel inquired of the Lord about what to do for the remaining tribe of Benjamin, as they swore not to give their daughters in marriage to them after the war.

- The tribes of Israel provide the two hundred surviving Benjaminite men with wives from the virgins of Jabesh-gilead.

- The men of Benjamin follow the advice and each takes a wife from the dancing women, returning to their own inheritance and rebuilding their cities.

- The book of Judges concludes by stating that "In those days, there was no king in Israel; everyone did what was right in his own eyes."

What stands out to you in this chapter?

Where do you see God in this chapter?

How have you been challenged while reading this chapter?

Any lingering thoughts or questions following the reading?

The Book of Galatians

Read Galatians 1   **Date** _____

Recap:

- Paul explains how so many people are already turning away from the true Gospel.

- We are to win the favor of God; not man.

- Paul declares that he has been crucified with Christ and no longer lives, but Christ lives in him.

What stands out to you in this chapter?

Where do you see God in this chapter?

How have you been challenged while reading this chapter?

Any lingering thoughts or questions following the reading?

ead Galatians 2   **Date** _____

ecap:

- Paul shares that he went up to Jerusalem after fourteen years to present the Gospel that he preached to the Gentiles to the leaders of the church.

- Paul recounts how he opposed Peter publicly in Antioch when Peter withdrew from eating with the Gentiles out of fear of the circumcision party.

- Paul reaffirms that he has been crucified with Christ, and it is no longer he who lives, but Christ who lives in him.

What stands out to you in this chapter?

Where do you see God in this chapter?

How have you been challenged while reading this chapter?

Any lingering thoughts or questions following the reading?

Read Galatians 3   **Date** _____

Recap:

- Paul asks the Galatians if they received the Spirit by works of the law or by hearing with faith, emphasizing that justification comes through faith in Christ, not by observing the law.

- Paul explains that those who have faith are blessed along with Abraham, wh is the father of all who believe.

- It is impossible to keep the whole law perfectly.

- Paul urges believers to put on Christ and to live in accordance with their new identity in Him.

What stands out to you in this chapter?

Where do you see God in this chapter?

How have you been challenged while reading this chapter?

Any lingering thoughts or questions following the reading?

ead Galatians 4   **Date** _____

ecap:

- Paul uses the analogy of a child and an heir to explain the difference between being under the law and being under faith in Christ.

- Paul reminds the Galatians that through faith in Christ, they have received the Spirit of adoption, and they can now call God "Abba, Father."

- Paul fears that his labor for the Galatians might have been in vain if they are now adopting a legalistic approach to their faith.

- Paul uses the story of Abraham's two sons, Ishmael and Isaac, born to Hagar and Sarah, to illustrate the difference between the children of promise and the children of the slave woman.

Vhat stands out to you in this chapter?

Vhere do you see God in this chapter?

Iow have you been challenged while reading this chapter?

ny lingering thoughts or questions following the reading?

Read Galatians 5   **Date** _____

Recap:

- Paul urges the Galatians to stand firm in the freedom that Christ has set them free and not to submit again to a yoke of slavery (the law).

- Paul emphasizes that in Christ Jesus, neither circumcision nor uncircumcisior counts for anything, but only faith working through love.

- Paul reminds the Galatians to serve one another in love, as the whole law is fulfilled in one word: "You shall love your neighbor as yourself."

- The battle of the flesh and the Spirit: Paul discusses the conflict between the flesh and the Spirit and encourages the Galatians to walk by the Spirit and no gratify the desires of the flesh.

- Paul urges the Galatians to crucify the flesh with its passions and desires and to live by the Spirit.

What stands out to you in this chapter?

Where do you see God in this chapter?

How have you been challenged while reading this chapter?

Any lingering thoughts or questions following the reading?

ead Galatians 6   **Date** _____

ecap:

- Paul urges the Galatians to restore someone caught in any transgression with a spirit of gentleness, considering themselves lest they too be tempted.

- Paul declares that he bears in his body the marks of Christ, signifying his devotion and service to the Lord.

- Paul concludes his letter with a benediction of grace, and sends greetings from himself and others with him.

What stands out to you in this chapter?

Where do you see God in this chapter?

How have you been challenged while reading this chapter?

Any lingering thoughts or questions following the reading?

The Book of 1 Samuel

Read 1 Samuel 1   **Date** _____

Recap:

- Elkanah, Hannah's husband, has two wives—Hannah and Peninnah. Peninnah ha: children, but Hannah is barren and deeply distressed because of her childlessness.

- Every year, the family travels to the tabernacle in Shiloh to worship and offer sacrifices. During one of these visits, Hannah goes to the tabernacle and prays fervently to the Lord, pouring out her heart and seeking His favor to grant her a sor

- Eli, the priest at the tabernacle, observes Hannah's silent prayer and, misunderstanding her distress, accuses her of being drunk. However, Hannah explains her situation to Eli, and he blesses her, praying that God would grant her request.

- She conceives and gives birth to a son whom she names Samuel, meaning "heard by God."

- Hannah keeps her promise to the Lord, dedicating Samuel to Him for his entire life.

What stands out to you in this chapter?

Where do you see God in this chapter?

How have you been challenged while reading this chapter?

Any lingering thoughts or questions following the reading?

Read 1 Samuel 2   **Date** _____

Recap:

- In her prayer praising God for her son (Samuel), Hannah emphasizes God's ability to lift up the lowly and bring down the mighty, showing His justice and righteous judgment.

- Eli's sons, Hophni and Phinehas, serve as priests at the tabernacle, but they are corrupt and disrespectful to God's offerings and laws.

- Samuel, on the other hand, serves faithfully as a child ministering before the Lord, wearing a linen ephod, a priestly garment.

- The Lord blesses Samuel's faithfulness, and he continues to grow in favor and stature both with God and with the people.

What stands out to you in this chapter?

Where do you see God in this chapter?

How have you been challenged while reading this chapter?

Any lingering thoughts or questions following the reading?

Read 1 Samuel 3   **Date** _____

Recap:

- God reveals Himself to Samuel and calls him to be a prophet, delivering messages from God to His people.

- The Lord informs Samuel of the judgment that will come upon Eli's house because of the sins of his sons, Hophni and Phinehas, and Eli's failure to restrain them.

- The prophecy predicts that both of Eli's sons will die on the same day, and God will cut off Eli's lineage as priests from serving at the tabernacle.

- Samuel, fearing to share this harsh message, keeps it to himself until morning when Eli asks him to reveal everything God had said.

- Samuel gains recognition as a prophet, and his reputation spreads throughout Israel, from Dan to Beersheba.

What stands out to you in this chapter?

Where do you see God in this chapter?

How have you been challenged while reading this chapter?

Any lingering thoughts or questions following the reading?

ead 1 Samuel 4   **Date** _____

ecap:

- The Israelites go to battle against the Philistines, hoping to overcome them with the presence of the Ark of the Covenant, which they bring from Shiloh.

- Seeking to secure their victory, the Israelites bring the Ark of the Covenant into the camp, believing it will protect them. But instead, the Philistines fought fiercely, capturing the Ark and killing Eli's two sons, Hophni and Phinehas, who were present at the battle.

- Upon hearing the news about the Ark, Eli falls backward from his seat and breaks his neck, dying at the age of ninety-eight.

- The Philistines suffer various plagues, including tumors, as a consequence of keeping the Ark.

What stands out to you in this chapter?

Where do you see God in this chapter?

How have you been challenged while reading this chapter?

Any lingering thoughts or questions following the reading?

Read 1 Samuel 5   **Date** _____

Recap:

- The Philistines take the Ark of the Covenant from Ashdod, where it had caused destruction and plagues, to the city of Gath.

- The Philistines decide to move the Ark to the city of Ekron, hoping to alleviat their afflictions, but the people there also cry out in distress.

- The decision is made to send the Ark back to Israel, acknowledging that they cannot endure the plagues brought upon them by God's presence.

- The Philistine rulers and priests prepare a cart to carry the Ark back to Israel, drawn by two cows that head straight to Beth-shemesh, an Israelite town, showing God's guidance in returning the Ark to its rightful place.

What stands out to you in this chapter?

Where do you see God in this chapter?

How have you been challenged while reading this chapter?

Any lingering thoughts or questions following the reading?

Read 1 Samuel 6   **Date** _____

Recap:

- The priests advise the Philistine's to return the Ark to the Israelites with a guilt offering to appease the God of Israel and seek His favor.
- The Philistine rulers prepare a chest made of gold, containing golden images of the tumors and rats that had afflicted them, and place it alongside the Ark as an offering of restitution.
- Some of the people of Beth-shemesh disrespect the Ark by looking into it, and as a consequence, God strikes down seventy men of the city.
- The people of Beth-shemesh, afraid of the Ark's presence and the loss of seventy men, send a message to the people of Kiriath-jearim, inviting them to take the Ark into their care.

What stands out to you in this chapter?

Where do you see God in this chapter?

How have you been challenged while reading this chapter?

Any lingering thoughts or questions following the reading?

Read 1 Samuel 7   **Date** _____

Recap:

- The Ark of the Covenant remains at Kiriath-jearim for twenty years after its return from the Philistines.

- During this time, Samuel serves as a judge and prophet among the people of Israel, calling them to turn back to the Lord and put away their foreign gods and idols.

- The Philistines gather to attack Israel, and the Israelites become afraid of their enemies.

- In response, Samuel leads the people in prayer and fasting, seeking God's intervention and help.

- The Lord answers their prayers and causes confusion among the Philistines. The Israelites are emboldened, and they defeat the Philistines in a great victory.

What stands out to you in this chapter?

Where do you see God in this chapter?

How have you been challenged while reading this chapter?

Any lingering thoughts or questions following the reading?

Read 1 Samuel 8   **Date** _____

Recap:

- As Samuel grows old, he appoints his sons as judges, but they prove to be corrupt and dishonest in their judgments.

- The elders of Israel approach Samuel in Ramah and express their dissatisfaction with his sons' leadership, demanding a king to rule over them like other nations.

- Samuel is frustrated by their request and seeks the Lord's guidance. God assures Samuel that it is not him they are rejecting but God Himself as their true King.

- God instructs Samuel to solemnly warn the people about the consequences of having a human king. He will take their sons for his armies, daughters for his service, tax their crops and livestock, and subject them to servitude.

What stands out to you in this chapter?

Where do you see God in this chapter?

How have you been challenged while reading this chapter?

Any lingering thoughts or questions following the reading?

Read 1 Samuel 9   **Date** _____

Recap:

- When Saul's father's donkeys go missing, Saul sets out on a search to find them, accompanied by one of his father's servants.

- Before Saul reaches the city where Samuel is, the Lord reveals to Samuel tha Saul will come to him, and he is to anoint Saul as the future king of Israel.

- As Saul approaches Samuel in the city gate, Samuel recognizes him as the one whom God has chosen to be king.

- Saul (now anointed King) is transformed and empowered by the Spirit of the Lord, becoming a new man, and the people around him take notice of this change.

What stands out to you in this chapter?

Where do you see God in this chapter?

How have you been challenged while reading this chapter?

Any lingering thoughts or questions following the reading?

ead 1 Samuel 10   **Date** _____

:ecap:

- Samuel, the prophet and judge of Israel, anoints Saul as the chosen king, marking the beginning of the monarchy in Israel

- After the anointing, Saul experiences a change of heart and is filled with the Spirit of God, gaining prophetic insights and abilities

- Samuel gives Saul three specific signs, including encounters with groups of prophets and symbolic events, all of which serve to confirm God's favor upon him as king

- Samuel gathers all the tribes of Israel, and through the casting of lots, Saul is chosen and confirmed as the king from the tribe of Benjamin

- Despite being anointed as king, Saul faces both supporters and doubters, and some individuals oppose his rule

What stands out to you in this chapter?

Where do you see God in this chapter?

How have you been challenged while reading this chapter?

Any lingering thoughts or questions following the reading?

Read 1 Samuel 11   **Date** _____

Recap:

- Nahash, the Ammonite king, threatens Jabesh Gilead, vowing to gouge out the right eye of every resident.

- The people of Jabesh Gilead request a seven-day grace period to seek help from other Israelite tribes.

- Saul, who had been anointed as king, hears about the distress in Jabesh Gilead and becomes filled with the Spirit of God in anger.

- Saul gathers an army and leads them in a surprise attack against the Ammonites, defeating them.

- The victory over the Ammonites confirms Saul's kingship in the eyes of the people.

- The people celebrate Saul's kingship at Gilgal through sacrifices and rejoicing.

What stands out to you in this chapter?

Where do you see God in this chapter?

How have you been challenged while reading this chapter?

Any lingering thoughts or questions following the reading?

ead 1 Samuel 12   **Date** _____

ecap:

- Samuel addresses the Israelites, reminding them of his just and righteous leadership.

- Samuel recounts his faithfulness and challenges the people to testify against him if he has done any wrong.

- The people admit their sin in asking for a king and express their desire to return to God's leadership.

- Samuel reassures the people that God will not abandon them if they obey His commands.

- Samuel calls upon God to send thunder and rain as a sign of His displeasure and the people's acknowledgement of their wrongdoing.

- The people are afraid and acknowledge their sin, asking Samuel to intercede for them with God.

- Samuel assures the people that he will continue to pray for them and teach them the way of righteousness.

What stands out to you in this chapter?

Where do you see God in this chapter?

How have you been challenged while reading this chapter?

Any lingering thoughts or questions following the reading?

Read 1 Samuel 13 **Date** _____

Recap:

- Saul reigned as king for two years over Israel.

- Saul chose 3,000 men from Israel, with 2,000 under his command and 1,00 under his son Jonathan's command.

- As Samuel's arrival was delayed, the Israelites grew impatient, and some soldiers began to desert.

- Samuel confronted Saul for his impatience and disobedience, stating that his kingdom would not endure because of his actions.

- Samuel announced that God had sought a man after His own heart to be king, implying that Saul was not that man.

- The Israelites with Saul and Jonathan were trembling with fear.

- The Lord saved Israel that day, and the battle continued beyond Beth-aven.

What stands out to you in this chapter?

Where do you see God in this chapter?

How have you been challenged while reading this chapter?

Any lingering thoughts or questions following the reading?

ead 1 Samuel 14   **Date** _____

ecap:

- Jonathan suggests that if the Philistines invite them to come up to their position, they will take it as a sign to attack.

- The Philistines call out to Jonathan and his armor-bearer, prompting them to climb up to the garrison. Jonathan takes it as a sign from God and proceeds with the attack.

- During the surprise attack, Jonathan and his armor-bearer kill about twenty Philistine soldiers, causing confusion and panic among the Philistine army.

- The Philistines become disoriented, attacking each other, and fleeing in chaos. God brings about a great victory for Israel that day.

- Saul admits his mistake and insists on continuing the pursuit of the Philistines until evening.

- Saul and his army have numerous battles with the Philistines and are successful in driving them away from Israel's territory.

What stands out to you in this chapter?

Where do you see God in this chapter?

How have you been challenged while reading this chapter?

Any lingering thoughts or questions following the reading?

Read 1 Samuel 15   **Date** _____

Recap:

- God instructs Saul to completely destroy the Amalekites, including men, women, children, and animals, as an act of judgment for their past sins against Israel.

- Saul and the Israelite army defeat the Amalekites but spare King Agag and the best of the livestock, disobeying God's command.

- God regrets making Saul king due to his disobedience and lack of complete loyalty to God's commands.

- Saul blames the people for sparing the best livestock, claiming they intended to sacrifice them to God, attempting to justify his actions.

- Samuel delivers a powerful rebuke to Saul, stating that obedience is more important to God than sacrifices, and God has rejected him as king.

- Samuel informs Saul that God has chosen a man after His own heart to be the new king over Israel, indicating the end of Saul's reign.

What stands out to you in this chapter?

Where do you see God in this chapter?

How have you been challenged while reading this chapter?

Any lingering thoughts or questions following the reading?

ead 1 Samuel 16   **Date** _____

ecap:

- Samuel grieves over God's rejection of Saul as king due to his disobedience and failure to carry out God's commands.

- God instructs Samuel to go to Bethlehem to anoint one of Jesse's sons as the new king of Israel.

- Jesse presents his seven sons before Samuel, starting with the eldest, Eliab. However, God does not choose any of them.

- When Samuel asks if there are any other sons, Jesse mentions David, who was tending the sheep. Samuel anoints David as the chosen king.

What stands out to you in this chapter?

Where do you see God in this chapter?

How have you been challenged while reading this chapter?

Any lingering thoughts or questions following the reading?

Read 1 Samuel 17   **Date** _____

Recap:

- Goliath, a giant champion from the Philistine army, challenges the Israelites to send a champion to fight him in single combat.

- Saul allows David to fight Goliath, but he tries to equip him with his own armor, which David declines, choosing to go with his sling and stones.

- Using his sling and stone, David strikes Goliath in the forehead, causing him to fall. David then finishes the Philistine giant with his own sword.

- Witnessing Goliath's defeat, the Philistines flee in fear, and the Israelites pursue and rout them in a great victory.

- David gains popularity among the people, and Saul appoints him as a commander in his army

What stands out to you in this chapter?

Where do you see God in this chapter?

How have you been challenged while reading this chapter?

Any lingering thoughts or questions following the reading?

Read 1 Samuel 18   **Date** _____

Recap:

- Saul takes David into his service and grows fond of him due to his military success. However, he becomes jealous and resentful of David's increasing popularity.

- Saul's jealousy intensifies to the point where he tries to kill David on multiple occasions. He makes David a commander in his army with the hope that he will be killed in battle.

- Saul gives his younger daughter Michal to David as a wife, hoping it will lead to David's downfall. However, Michal loves David and helps him escape Saul's assassination attempts.

- David continues to be victorious in his military actions.

What stands out to you in this chapter?

Where do you see God in this chapter?

How have you been challenged while reading this chapter?

Any lingering thoughts or questions following the reading?

Read 1 Samuel 19   **Date** _____

Recap:

- Jonathan, who deeply cares for David, warns him about Saul's plan and advises him to hide until he can speak with Saul.

- David flees to Samuel in Naioth, and Saul sends messengers after him. However, when they encounter a group of prophets prophesying, the Spirit of God comes upon them, and they end up prophesying as well.

- Jonathan devises a plan to determine Saul's intentions towards David and promises to inform David of the outcome.

- Jonathan confirms Saul's malicious intentions towards David, prompting David to flee and leading to a tearful parting between the two friends.

What stands out to you in this chapter?

Where do you see God in this chapter?

How have you been challenged while reading this chapter?

Any lingering thoughts or questions following the reading?

ead 1 Samuel 20   **Date** _____

ecap:

- Jonathan vows to find out if Saul truly intends to harm David and promises to inform him of the outcome.

- Jonathan devises a plan to determine Saul's feelings towards David during the feast and sends a signal to inform David of the results.

- During the feast, Saul becomes enraged at David's absence and publicly expresses his anger, revealing his hostility towards him.

- Jonathan uses the agreed-upon signal to warn David of Saul's intentions, signaling that he must flee for his safety.

- David and Jonathan's plan is executed as planned, and David evades Saul's pursuit.

What stands out to you in this chapter?

Where do you see God in this chapter?

How have you been challenged while reading this chapter?

Any lingering thoughts or questions following the reading?

Read 1 Samuel 21   **Date** _____

Recap:

- Fleeing from Saul, David goes to Nob, seeking help from Ahimelech the priest.

- Ahimelech gives David the consecrated bread from the tabernacle since ther wasn't any common bread available, and he also provides David with Goliath's sword.

- Not feeling safe in Nob, David travels to Gath, seeking refuge among the Philistines.

- Fearful of being recognized, David pretends to be insane before King Achish of Gath to avoid capture.

- As David hides in the cave of Adullam, many distressed, discontented, and indebted people join him, becoming his followers.

- Saul confronts Ahimelech about assisting David and accuses him of conspiring against him.

What stands out to you in this chapter?

Where do you see God in this chapter?

How have you been challenged while reading this chapter?

Any lingering thoughts or questions following the reading?

Read 1 Samuel 22   **Date** _____

Recap:

- David, still fleeing from Saul's pursuit, takes refuge in the cave of Adullam. His family and others join him, forming a band of about four hundred men.

- Saul learns that Ahimelech the priest had assisted David, and he accuses Ahimelech and the priests of conspiring against him.

- Saul orders Doeg to kill Ahimelech and the other priests, but Doeg kills eighty-five priests, along with men, women, children, and livestock in the city of Nob.

What stands out to you in this chapter?

Where do you see God in this chapter?

How have you been challenged while reading this chapter?

Any lingering thoughts or questions following the reading?

Read 1 Samuel 23   **Date** _____

Recap:

- Upon learning that the Philistines were attacking Keilah, David inquires of the Lord and, with God's approval, leads his men to rescue the people of Keilah.

- David seeks the Lord's guidance to know if the people of Keilah will betray him to Saul, and the Lord advises him to leave the city to avoid Saul's capture.

- Jonathan visits David in the wilderness of Ziph and strengthens his faith in God, reassuring him that he will become king and that Jonathan will be second to him in the kingdom.

- Saul and his army pursue David and surround him and his men in the wilderness of Maon.

- Just as Saul is about to capture David, the Philistines launch an attack on Israel, causing Saul to leave and return to defend his own land.

- David takes advantage of Saul's departure and flees to the stronghold of Engedi, evading Saul's pursuit.

- Saul acknowledges that David will become king and requests that David spare his descendants once he is established as king.

What stands out to you in this chapter?

Where do you see God in this chapter?

How have you been challenged while reading this chapter?

Any lingering thoughts or questions following the reading?

ead 1 Samuel 24   **Date** _____

ecap:

- While Saul is pursuing David in the wilderness of En-gedi, David has the opportunity to kill Saul, but he refrains from harming God's anointed king.

- After Saul relieves himself in a cave, David emerges and confronts him from a distance, revealing that he could have killed Saul but chose not to.

- David pleads with Saul, questioning why he is pursuing him and asserting his innocence and loyalty.

- Saul admits his wrongdoing and recognizes that David is more righteous than he is, acknowledging that David spared his life.

- Saul prophesies that David will be king and that his own kingdom will not endure, showing a realization of God's will.

- Saul acknowledges that David will become king, and he withdraws his pursuit for the time being.

What stands out to you in this chapter?

Where do you see God in this chapter?

How have you been challenged while reading this chapter?

Any lingering thoughts or questions following the reading?

Read 1 Samuel 25   **Date** _____

Recap:

- David sends messengers to Nabal, a wealthy man from Maon, requesting provisions as a gesture of goodwill.

- Nabal responds harshly to David's request, insulting him and refusing to offe any provisions.

- Abigail quickly gathers a generous offering of food and supplies, and withou David listens to Abigail and recognizes the wisdom in her words, deciding tc spare Nabal and his household from harm.

- The next morning, Abigail tells Nabal about her intervention with David, and he becomes paralyzed with shock. About ten days later, the Lord strikes Nabal, and he dies.

- After Nabal's death, David sends messengers to propose marriage to Abigail, a

What stands out to you in this chapter?

Where do you see God in this chapter?

How have you been challenged while reading this chapter?

Any lingering thoughts or questions following the reading?

Read 1 Samuel 26   **Date** _____

Recap:

- Saul continues to pursue David with an army to capture and kill him.

- David and Abishai find Saul and his army camped, with Saul sleeping in the middle of the camp and his spear stuck in the ground near his head.

- Abishai suggests killing Saul with his own spear while he sleeps, but David refuses, showing his continued respect for God's anointed king.

- From a safe distance, David calls out to Abner, the commander of Saul's army, to end the pursuit and avoid more bloodshed.

- Saul recognizes David's voice and acknowledges that David is more righteous than he is, showing remorse for his pursuit of David.

- Saul begs David to spare his life and vows not to continue pursuing him.

- Saul recognizes his defeat and returns home, ending his pursuit of David for the time being.

What stands out to you in this chapter?

Where do you see God in this chapter?

How have you been challenged while reading this chapter?

Any lingering thoughts or questions following the reading?

Read 1 Samuel 27   **Date** _____

Recap:

- David decides to seek refuge with King Achish of Gath, a Philistine city.

- While living in Ziklag, David conducts raids against the Geshurites, the Girzites, and the Amalekites, preventing them from raiding Israelite territories

- When King Achish inquires about David's raids, David lies, claiming he has been raiding against Israelite towns instead of their common enemies.

- Achish believes David's deception and thinks he has turned against Israel completely, trusting him as a loyal servant.

- Despite the dangerous circumstances, David manages to protect himself and his men while living among the Philistines.

What stands out to you in this chapter?

Where do you see God in this chapter?

How have you been challenged while reading this chapter?

Any lingering thoughts or questions following the reading?

ead 1 Samuel 28   **Date** _____

ecap:

- As the Philistine armies gather to fight against Israel, Saul becomes greatly afraid and desperate for guidance from the Lord.
- When Saul inquires of the Lord for guidance, God does not answer him through dreams, prophets, or the Urim, leaving Saul in distress.
- Saul disguises himself and goes to the medium at night so that he won't be recognized.
- The medium successfully summoned Samuel's spirit, and he appears before Saul.
- Samuel rebukes Saul for his disobedience
- Saul is deeply troubled by Samuel's words, and his strength leaves him due to the severity of the message.

What stands out to you in this chapter?

Where do you see God in this chapter?

How have you been challenged while reading this chapter?

Any lingering thoughts or questions following the reading?

Read 1 Samuel 29   **Date** _____

Recap:

- The Philistine commanders are wary of David's presence in their army, fearing he might turn against them during the battle.

- King Achish vouches for David's loyalty, stating that he has found no fault in him since he joined his ranks.

- David and his men return to Ziklag, finding the city burned down and their families taken captive by the Amalekites during their absence.

- David seeks the Lord's guidance through prayer.

- David's leadership and faithfulness are affirmed by God's deliverance, further solidifying his position as a respected leader among his followers.

What stands out to you in this chapter?

Where do you see God in this chapter?

How have you been challenged while reading this chapter?

Any lingering thoughts or questions following the reading?

Read 1 Samuel 30   **Date** _____

Recap:

- While David and his men were away with the Philistine army, the Amalekites attacked Ziklag, burning it down and taking captive all the women and children, including David's two wives, Ahinoam and Abigail.

- David's men are so distraught over the loss of their families that they turn against him, blaming him for the tragedy.

- With the Lord's direction, David and his men set out to pursue the Amalekites, determined to rescue their families.

- David and his men launch a successful attack on the Amalekites, recovering their families and all the possessions that had been taken.

- David's leadership is once again affirmed as his men acknowledge his wisdom and fairness in the distribution of the spoils.

What stands out to you in this chapter?

Where do you see God in this chapter?

How have you been challenged while reading this chapter?

Any lingering thoughts or questions following the reading?

Read 1 Samuel 31   **Date** _____

Recap:

- The Philistines engage in battle against Israel, resulting in a heavy defeat for the Israelites, which included the deaths of Saul's sons, including Jonathan, Abinadab, and Malchishua.

- Fearing torture and humiliation at the hands of the Philistines, Saul asks his armor-bearer to kill him with his sword.

- The armor-bearer is too afraid to carry out Saul's request, so Saul falls on his own sword, taking his own life.

- The Philistines decapitate Saul's body and fasten his corpse to the wall of the Philistine city of Beth-shan as a sign of their triumph.

- With Saul's death, his reign as king over Israel comes to an end, and the stage is set for David to become the new king.

What stands out to you in this chapter?

Where do you see God in this chapter?

How have you been challenged while reading this chapter?

Any lingering thoughts or questions following the reading?

The Book of 1 Peter

Read 1 Peter 1   **Date** _____

Recap:

- Peter starts by praising God for His abundant mercy, which has given believers a living hope through the resurrection of Jesus Christ from the dead.

- Peter reminds the readers that their inheritance in heaven is imperishable, undefiled, and unfading, kept for them by God's power.

- Peter acknowledges that though believers may face trials and sufferings, their faith will be proven genuine and result in praise, glory, and honor at the revelation of Jesus Christ.

- Peter encourages the readers to rejoice in their salvation, even in the midst of trials, because they are receiving the outcome of their faith - the salvation of their souls.

What stands out to you in this chapter?

Where do you see God in this chapter?

How have you been challenged while reading this chapter?

Any lingering thoughts or questions following the reading?

Read 1 Peter 2   **Date** _____

Recap:

- Peter urges believers to put away all malice, deceit, hypocrisy, envy, and slander, and to long for pure spiritual milk, that they may grow in their salvation.

- Peter reminds believers that they were once not a people, but now they are God's people, once without mercy, but now they have received mercy.

- Peter urges believers to abstain from the passions of the flesh, which wage war against their souls.

- Peter explains that Christ bore our sins in His body on the tree, so that we might die to sin and live for righteousness.

- Peter encourages believers to follow Christ's example of humility, not repaying evil for evil but entrusting themselves to God.

What stands out to you in this chapter?

Where do you see God in this chapter?

How have you been challenged while reading this chapter?

Any lingering thoughts or questions following the reading?

Read 1 Peter 3   **Date** _____

Recap:

- Peter instructs wives to be submissive to their own husbands, even if their husbands are not believers, with the hope of winning them over by their conduct.

- Peter points to the example of holy women in the past, like Sarah, who trusted in God and were submissive to their husbands.

- Husbands are to honor their wives and to treat them with understanding and respect, as co-heirs of the grace of life.

- All believers are to live righteously, not repaying evil for evil, but seeking to do good and to be a blessing to others.

- All believers are to have unity of mind, sympathy, brotherly love, a tender heart, and a humble mind.

- Peter advises believers to turn away from evil and do good, seeking peace with others.

What stands out to you in this chapter?

Where do you see God in this chapter?

How have you been challenged while reading this chapter?

Any lingering thoughts or questions following the reading?

Read 1 Peter 4   **Date** _____

Recap:

- Peter urges believers to arm themselves with the same mindset as Christ, being prepared to suffer for righteousness' sake.

- Believers are to live the rest of their lives no longer in the fleshly desires but according to God's will.

- Believers are to be fervent in love, showing hospitality to one another withou grumbling.

- Suffering in the flesh serves to equip believers to live for the will of God and not for human passions.

- Peter advises believers not to be surprised at the fiery trial when it comes upon them, but to rejoice in sharing Christ's sufferings.

What stands out to you in this chapter?

Where do you see God in this chapter?

How have you been challenged while reading this chapter?

Any lingering thoughts or questions following the reading?

ead 1 Peter 5   **Date** _____

ecap:

- Elders among the believers should shepherd the flock of God willingly, not for personal gain but with a sincere heart.

- Peter urges believers to cast all their anxieties on God because He cares for them.

- Believers are to resist the devil, standing firm in their faith, knowing that their brothers and sisters throughout the world are facing similar sufferings.

What stands out to you in this chapter?

Where do you see God in this chapter?

How have you been challenged while reading this chapter?

Any lingering thoughts or questions following the reading?

The Book of 2 Peter

Read 2 Peter 1   **Date** _____

Recap:

- Just like Paul, you and me, Peter is also a slave to Jesus Christ.

- God's divine power is everything we'll ever need in our lives.

- Peter urges believers to be diligent to confirm their calling and election, as this will keep them from stumbling.

- Peter emphasizes that no prophecy came from human will but was carried along by the Holy Spirit, speaking from God.

- Peter warns that just as there were false prophets in the past, there will be false teachers among them who will bring destructive heresies.

- Peter assures that judgment awaits false teachers, as it did for the rebellious angels and the ancient world.

What stands out to you in this chapter?

Where do you see God in this chapter?

How have you been challenged while reading this chapter?

Any lingering thoughts or questions following the reading?

Read 2 Peter 2   **Date** _____

Recap:

- Peter warns that just as there were false prophets in the past, there will be false teachers among them who will bring destructive heresies.

- Peter assures that judgment awaits false teachers, as it did for the rebellious angels and the ancient world.

- God knows how to rescue the godly from trials while keeping the unrighteous under punishment for the day of judgment.

- Peter describes false teachers as arrogant and blasphemous, indulging in sensual pleasures, and enticing others with sinful desires.

- Peter warns that false teachers promise freedom, but they themselves are slaves of corruption.

What stands out to you in this chapter?

Where do you see God in this chapter?

How have you been challenged while reading this chapter?

Any lingering thoughts or questions following the reading?

Read 2 Peter 3   **Date** _____

Recap:

- In the last days, scoffers will come, mocking the promise of Christ's return, saying, "Where is the promise of His coming?"

- Peter explains that the Lord's delay in His return is due to His patience, desiring that none should perish, but all should come to repentance.

- The day of the Lord is coming like a thief, in which the heavens will pass away with a roar, and the elements will be burned and dissolved.

- Peter looks forward to the promise of a new heavens and a new earth, where righteousness dwells.

What stands out to you in this chapter?

Where do you see God in this chapter?

How have you been challenged while reading this chapter?

Any lingering thoughts or questions following the reading?

The Book of 2 Samuel

ead 2 Samuel 1

ecap:

- Amalekite claims to have killed him to end his suffering.

- Instead of honoring the Amalekite for supposedly killing Saul, David orders his men to execute the Amalekite for admitting to killing the Lord's anointed.

- David composes a heartfelt lament for Saul and Jonathan, expressing his sorrow and respect for the fallen king and his dear friend.

- Despite the loss of Saul and Jonathan, David's anointing as king marks the beginning of his reign and establishes him as the chosen leader of Israel.

What stands out to you in this chapter?

Where do you see God in this chapter?

How have you been challenged while reading this chapter?

Any lingering thoughts or questions following the reading?

Read 2 Samuel 2   **Date** _____

Recap:

- The reigns of David and Ish-bosheth lead to a period of conflict between the respective houses, as each asserts their claim to the throne.

- Asahel, one of David's mighty men and Joab's brother, relentlessly pursues Abner but is killed by Abner in self-defense.

- Joab agrees to a truce but secretly seeks revenge for Asahel's death.

- He lures Abner back and kills him, avenging his brother.

- David expresses deep sorrow over Abner's death, disavowing any involvement and declaring a curse upon Joab and his family.

What stands out to you in this chapter?

Where do you see God in this chapter?

How have you been challenged while reading this chapter?

Any lingering thoughts or questions following the reading?

Read 2 Samuel 3   **Date** _____

Recap:

- Abner meets with David and proposes to bring all of Israel under David's rule, promising to persuade the elders and people to support him as king.

- Joab, David's commander, is suspicious of Abner's intentions and takes matters into his own hands. He kills Abner in revenge for his brother Asahel's death.

- David mourns Abner's death and publicly condemns Joab and his actions, affirming his innocence in the matter.

- David is deeply troubled by the assassination of Ish-bosheth and orders the execution of the two captains responsible for the act.

- The people of Israel recognize David as their rightful king, and he makes a covenant with them, solidifying his rule.

What stands out to you in this chapter?

Where do you see God in this chapter?

How have you been challenged while reading this chapter?

Any lingering thoughts or questions following the reading?

Read 2 Samuel 4   **Date** _____

Recap:

- After killing Ish-bosheth, Baanah and Rechab cut off his head and bring it to David in Hebron, thinking that David would reward them for their deed.

- David orders the execution of Baanah and Rechab as punishment for their crime, showing that he does not condone the use of violence to gain political advantage.

- With the death of Ish-bosheth and the execution of his murderers, the house of Saul loses its claim to the throne, and David's rule over all Israel becomes firmly established.

What stands out to you in this chapter?

Where do you see God in this chapter?

How have you been challenged while reading this chapter?

Any lingering thoughts or questions following the reading?

ead 2 Samuel 5   **Date** _____

ecap:

- After becoming king, David sets out to conquer the Jebusite city of Jerusalem, which had been an unconquered stronghold.

- He successfully captures the city and establishes it as his capital.

- With God's guidance, David continues to have success against the Philistines and other enemies of Israel, solidifying his rule and expanding the kingdom's borders.

- God establishes a covenant with David, promising to build him a house and to establish his kingdom forever.

What stands out to you in this chapter?

Where do you see God in this chapter?

How have you been challenged while reading this chapter?

Any lingering thoughts or questions following the reading?

Read 2 Samuel 6   **Date** _____

Recap:

- David leads a procession to bring the Ark of the Covenant from the house of Obed-edom to the City of David (Jerusalem).

- As the Ark is being transported on a cart, the oxen stumble, and Uzzah instinctively reaches out to steady the Ark. God struck Uzzah dead.

- David becomes afraid of the Lord after Uzzah's death and decides not to bring the Ark into the City of David. Instead, he takes it to the house of Obed-edom the Gittite.

- After hearing about the blessings on Obed-edom's house, David decides to make another attempt to bring the Ark to Jerusalem.

- David and the people transport the Ark with great reverence and celebration.

- As the Ark is brought into Jerusalem, David dances with all his might before the Lord, wearing a linen ephod, expressing his joy and reverence for God.

What stands out to you in this chapter?

Where do you see God in this chapter?

How have you been challenged while reading this chapter?

Any lingering thoughts or questions following the reading?

Read 2 Samuel 7   **Date** _____

Recap:

- David expresses his desire to build a permanent dwelling place, a "house," for the Ark of the Covenant and for the Lord.

- Through Nathan, God tells David that He will not have him build a house, but instead, God will establish a house, a dynasty, for David.

- God promises David that He will raise up one of his descendants to sit on the throne after him, and this descendant will build a house for God's name.

- God assures David that He will establish the throne of his kingdom forever, promising an eternal dynasty.

- Over the generations, the promise made to David is fulfilled through the establishment of the Davidic dynasty and, ultimately, the birth of Jesus, who is from the line of David.

What stands out to you in this chapter?

Where do you see God in this chapter?

How have you been challenged while reading this chapter?

Any lingering thoughts or questions following the reading?

Read 2 Samuel 8   **Date** _____

Recap:

- David defeats the Philistines and takes control of their major cities, including Gath and Metheg-ammah.

- As a result of his military conquests and the tribute from defeated nations, David accumulates vast amounts of wealth, including gold, silver, and valuable items.

- David dedicates the gold and silver from the conquered nations to the Lord, acknowledging God's role in his victories.

- David's reputation as a victorious and capable leader grows, and the Lord gives him success in all his endeavors.

What stands out to you in this chapter?

Where do you see God in this chapter?

How have you been challenged while reading this chapter?

Any lingering thoughts or questions following the reading?

Read 2 Samuel 9   Date _____

Recap:

- After becoming king over all Israel, David expresses his desire to show kindness to any remaining member of Saul's household for the sake of his dear friend Jonathan.

- David sends for Mephibosheth and invites him to come to Jerusalem, assuring him that he will be treated kindly.

- Mephibosheth, fearing for his life and expecting judgment, humbly bows before David and acknowledges himself as David's servant.

- Instead of punishing Mephibosheth, David shows him great kindness by restoring all the land that belonged to Saul, ensuring that Mephibosheth would have provisions and servants to tend to the land.

- Mephibosheth expresses his deep gratitude to David for showing him kindness, acknowledging that he is unworthy of such favor.

What stands out to you in this chapter?

Where do you see God in this chapter?

How have you been challenged while reading this chapter?

Any lingering thoughts or questions following the reading?

Read 2 Samuel 10   **Date** _____

Recap:

- David learns about the mistreatment of his delegation and the Ammonite-Syrian alliance. He sends Joab, his army commander, with the entire army to confront them.

- After their defeat by Israel, the Syrians realize that they are no match for David's forces and make peace with Israel, becoming their subjects.

- When the Ammonites see that the Arameans have been defeated, they withdraw into their fortified cities.

- Other victories are mentioned that David's armies achieved against various nations.

What stands out to you in this chapter?

Where do you see God in this chapter?

How have you been challenged while reading this chapter?

Any lingering thoughts or questions following the reading?

Read 2 Samuel 11   **Date** _____

Recap:

- David sees Bathsheba, the wife of Uriah the Hittite, bathing, and he gets the hots for her.

- Despite knowing that Bathsheba is married, David sends for her and commits adultery with her, and she becomes pregnant.

- When David realizes that Bathsheba is pregnant, he attempts to cover up his sin by bringing Uriah back from the battlefront and encouraging him to spend time with his wife.

- Uriah, devoted to his duty as a soldier, refuses to go home and be with his wife while his fellow soldiers are still fighting.

- Frustrated by Uriah's loyalty, David sends a letter to Joab, the commander of his army, instructing him to place Uriah in a dangerous position in battle, resulting in his death.

- Uriah is killed in battle according to David's plan.

- After a period of mourning, David takes Bathsheba as his wife.

What stands out to you in this chapter?

Where do you see God in this chapter?

How have you been challenged while reading this chapter?

Any lingering thoughts or questions following the reading?

Read 2 Samuel 12   **Date** _____

Recap:

- Nathan reveals to David that he is the rich man in the parable, and he has committed a great sin by taking Bathsheba and orchestrating Uriah's death.

- Confronted with his sin, David confesses his wrongdoing and acknowledges that he has sinned against the Lord.

- Nathan tells David that the Lord has forgiven his sin but that there will still be severe consequences: the child conceived with Bathsheba will die.

- As prophesied, the child becomes seriously sick and dies despite David's fasting and pleading with the Lord.

- After the child's death, David stops mourning and worships the Lord, recognizing God's sovereignty and justice.

- Bathsheba conceives again, and she gives birth to a son named Solomon, whom the Lord loves.

What stands out to you in this chapter?

Where do you see God in this chapter?

How have you been challenged while reading this chapter?

Any lingering thoughts or questions following the reading?

ead 2 Samuel 13   **Date** _____

ecap:

- When Tamar comes to care for Amnon, he seizes the opportunity and rapes her against her will.

- Tamar tearfully laments her violation, and Absalom, her brother, comforts her.

- Absalom eventually carries out his plan for revenge and has Amnon killed during a feast.

- Upon hearing the news of Amnon's death, David mourns deeply for his son.

- Despite the tragic circumstances, David longs for Absalom to return, as his grief over Amnon's death is overshadowed by his love for Absalom.

What stands out to you in this chapter?

Where do you see God in this chapter?

How have you been challenged while reading this chapter?

Any lingering thoughts or questions following the reading?

Read 2 Samuel 14   **Date** _____

Recap:

- The woman from Tekoa comes before David disguised as a mourner and pleads with him for justice regarding a situation involving her two sons. She uses her story to appeal to David's sense of mercy and reconciliation.

- David is touched by the woman's story and agrees to protect her son, ensuring that he will not be harmed.

- The wise woman then reveals her true identity and Joab's involvement in the plan, showing David that the whole scenario was crafted to bring about Absalom's return.

- David heeds the woman's advice and allows Absalom to return to Jerusalem. However, David refuses to see Absalom face to face.

What stands out to you in this chapter?

Where do you see God in this chapter?

How have you been challenged while reading this chapter?

Any lingering thoughts or questions following the reading?

Read 2 Samuel 15   **Date** _____

Recap:

- Absalom starts to conspire against his father David, seeking to take the throne for himself.

- Absalom wins the hearts of the people by acting kindly and empathetic towards them, convincing them that he would bring about better justice and governance than David.

- Many people in Israel join Absalom's rebellion, including some of David's key advisors and officials.

- David flees from Jerusalem to avoid confrontation and protect the city.

- Despite the difficult circumstances, David continues to place his trust in God, seeking His guidance and protection during this time of crisis.

What stands out to you in this chapter?

Where do you see God in this chapter?

How have you been challenged while reading this chapter?

Any lingering thoughts or questions following the reading?

Read 2 Samuel 16   **Date** _____

Recap:

- As David and his followers continue their journey, Shimei, a member of Saul's family, comes out and curses David, throwing stones at him and his men.

- Despite the hurtful accusations and insults, David shows humility and restraint, refusing to retaliate against Shimei or his men.

- Ahithophel advises Absalom to publicly take David's concubines and thus assert his dominance over his father's household. This act would also demonstrate to the people of Israel that there is no chance of reconciliation with David.

What stands out to you in this chapter?

Where do you see God in this chapter?

How have you been challenged while reading this chapter?

Any lingering thoughts or questions following the reading?

ead 2 Samuel 17   **Date** _____

ecap:

- Feeling humiliated, Ahithophel goes home, puts his affairs in order, and hangs himself.

- David and his followers cross the Jordan River and find a safe place to hide, escaping Absalom's forces.

- As David hides, many people from various tribes of Israel come to join him and offer their support.

- David and his followers cross the Jordan River under the cover of darkness and continue to evade Absalom's forces.

What stands out to you in this chapter?

Where do you see God in this chapter?

How have you been challenged while reading this chapter?

Any lingering thoughts or questions following the reading?

Read 2 Samuel 18   **Date** _____

Recap:

- David organizes his troops and appoints commanders to lead the army against Absalom's forces, instructing them to deal gently with Absalom for h sake.

- David's army prevails in the battle, and Absalom's forces suffer heavy casualties. Many of Absalom's soldiers are killed in the forest.

- Upon finding Absalom trapped, Joab's soldiers are hesitant to harm him because of David's command to deal gently with Absalom.

- However, Joab takes matters into his own hands and kills Absalom by thrusting three javelins into his heart.

- When David learns of Absalom's death, he is deeply saddened and mourns the loss of his son, expressing his sorrow in tears and lamentation.

What stands out to you in this chapter?

Where do you see God in this chapter?

How have you been challenged while reading this chapter?

Any lingering thoughts or questions following the reading?

ead 2 Samuel 19   **Date** _____

ecap:

- Despite the victory of his army and the end of the rebellion, David is overcome with grief over the loss of his son Absalom.

- Joab, David's commander, confronts him for his excessive mourning, reminding him that his actions are causing demoralization among his troops, who fought for him at the risk of their lives.

- David heeds Joab's advice and returns to Jerusalem, putting an end to his mourning and resuming his duties as king.

- Despite the internal divisions, David is eventually reinstated as king over all Israel, and the people of Judah and Israel unite under his rule.

What stands out to you in this chapter?

Where do you see God in this chapter?

How have you been challenged while reading this chapter?

Any lingering thoughts or questions following the reading?

Read 2 Samuel 20   **Date** _____

Recap:

- A man named Sheba, from the tribe of Benjamin, leads a rebellion against David, refusing to acknowledge his kingship over Israel.

- Joab resumes his position as commander of the Israelite army and leads the troops to pursue Sheba.

- The people of Abel Beth Maacah throw Sheba's head over the wall, bringing an end to the rebellion.

What stands out to you in this chapter?

Where do you see God in this chapter?

How have you been challenged while reading this chapter?

Any lingering thoughts or questions following the reading?

ead 2 Samuel 21   **Date** _____

ecap:

- There is a severe famine in the land of Israel for three years, and when David seeks the Lord's guidance, he is informed that the famine is a result of Saul's earlier sin against the Gibeonites.

- David approaches the Gibeonites and asks them what should be done to make amends for Saul's actions.

- The Gibeonites demand that seven of Saul's descendants be handed over to them to be executed as retribution for Saul's crimes against them.

- David agrees to the Gibeonites' demand and hands over seven descendants of Saul, including five of his sons and two of his grandsons, for execution.

- These sons were hanged and left exposed as a sign of judgment.

- More battles are spoken of as the chapter goes on and concludes.

What stands out to you in this chapter?

Where do you see God in this chapter?

How have you been challenged while reading this chapter?

Any lingering thoughts or questions following the reading?

Read 2 Samuel 22   **Date** _____

Recap:

- David calls the Lord as his rock, fortress, and deliverer, recognizing God's power and protection in times of trouble.

- David acknowledges how the Lord delivered him from powerful and mighty enemies, rescuing him from the hands of those who sought to harm him.

- David acknowledges that God's guidance and strength enabled him to overcome his enemies, making him as swift as a deer and enabling him to scale walls.

- The song concludes with David expressing gratitude for God's steadfast love and faithfulness, proclaiming that the Lord is the source of his strength and victory.

What stands out to you in this chapter?

Where do you see God in this chapter?

How have you been challenged while reading this chapter?

Any lingering thoughts or questions following the reading?

Read 2 Samuel 23   **Date** _____

Recap:

- The chapter begins with "these are the last words of David," suggesting that what follows is a collection of David's final reflections and wisdom.

- David proclaims that the Lord spoke through him, saying that the ruler of Israel must be just and fear God, resembling the light of the morning without clouds, shining on a bright day.

- The chapter goes on to highlight the heroic deeds of other members of David's elite group of warriors, such as Abishai, Benaiah, and others, who demonstrated their unwavering loyalty and bravery in defending their king.

What stands out to you in this chapter?

Where do you see God in this chapter?

How have you been challenged while reading this chapter?

Any lingering thoughts or questions following the reading?

Read 2 Samuel 24   **Date** _____

Recap:

- The chapter begins with David's decision to take a census of the people of Israel and Judah. This act is not viewed favorably in the Bible, as it suggests a lack of trust in God's provision and a desire for self-reliance.

- Joab, David's commander, expresses his disapproval of the census, warning David that it may lead to God's judgment against Israel.

- After the census is completed, David becomes conscience-stricken and realizes the gravity of his sin. God, angered by David's pride and disobedience, sends the prophet Gad to deliver a message of judgment.

- Gad offers David three choices of punishment: seven years of famine, three months of fleeing from his enemies, or three days of pestilence in the land.

- God sends a severe pestilence upon Israel, resulting in the deaths of 70,000 men.

- God stops the destruction and commands the angel to withdraw.

- David, upon witnessing the devastation caused by the plague, repents and pleads with God to spare the people.

What stands out to you in this chapter?

Where do you see God in this chapter?

How have you been challenged while reading this chapter?

Any lingering thoughts or questions following the reading?

The Book of 1 John

ead 1 John 1   **Date** _____

ecap:

- Word of Life, which is Jesus Christ, the eternal life that was with the Father and was made manifest to humanity.

- John emphasizes the invitation to have fellowship with God and with one another, as believers walk in the light, where there is no darkness.

- If believers confess their sins, God is faithful and just to forgive and cleanse them from all unrighteousness.

What stands out to you in this chapter?

Where do you see God in this chapter?

How have you been challenged while reading this chapter?

Any lingering thoughts or questions following the reading?

Read 1 John 2   **Date** _____

Recap:

- We are to come to know God better by keeping His commands.

- We are not to love the world; be in it, but not of it.

- No lie will ever come from the "truth" of God's word.

- These verses are so important, as false teachers are trying to lead us astray.

What stands out to you in this chapter?

Where do you see God in this chapter?

How have you been challenged while reading this chapter?

Any lingering thoughts or questions following the reading?

Read 1 John 3   **Date** _____

Recap:

- Followers of God have earned the right to be called "Children of God."

- John is showing us that some will profess Christ, but go on sinning and not repenting of their sin; showing their true nature, as not a follower of Christ.

- Christ laid down His life for believers, and they should also be willing to lay down their lives for one another.

What stands out to you in this chapter?

Where do you see God in this chapter?

How have you been challenged while reading this chapter?

Any lingering thoughts or questions following the reading?

Read 1 John 4   **Date** _____

Recap:

- John affirms that those who belong to God listen to the apostles and have the Spirit of God within them.

- John reiterates the command to love one another, as God's love abides in those who love and know Him.

- John assures believers that God's love is perfected in those who abide in Him, and they can have confidence in the day of judgment.

- John explains that perfect love casts out fear, and those who fear have not been perfected in love.

What stands out to you in this chapter?

Where do you see God in this chapter?

How have you been challenged while reading this chapter?

Any lingering thoughts or questions following the reading?

ead 1 John 5   **Date** _____

ecap:

- John assures believers that God has given them eternal life, and this life is in His Son.

- John advises that there is a sin leading to death, for which he does not recommend prayer, but for any other sin, believers can pray for forgiveness.

- John emphasizes that everyone born of God overcomes the world, and this victory comes through their faith.

What stands out to you in this chapter?

Where do you see God in this chapter?

How have you been challenged while reading this chapter?

Any lingering thoughts or questions following the reading?

The Book of 2 John

Read 2 John 1   **Date** _____

Recap:

- The elder warns the recipients of the letter to watch out for deceivers who dc not confess the coming of Jesus Christ in the flesh.

- The elder encourages the recipients to abide in the teaching of Christ, emphasizing that those who abide in it have both the Father and the Son.

What stands out to you in this chapter?

Where do you see God in this chapter?

How have you been challenged while reading this chapter?

Any lingering thoughts or questions following the reading?

The Book of 3 John

ead 3 John 1   **Date** _____

ecap:

- The elder praises some brethren who have reported about Gaius' love and hospitality.

- The elder encourages Gaius to imitate what is good, indicating that the one who does good is of God.

- The elder expresses his desire to see Gaius in person and conveys greetings from friends.

What stands out to you in this chapter?

Where do you see God in this chapter?

How have you been challenged while reading this chapter?

Any lingering thoughts or questions following the reading?

The Book of Lamentations

Read Lamentations 1   **Date** _____

Recap:

- Lamentations begins with a depiction of the once glorious city of Jerusalem, now deserted and in ruins after the destruction by the Babylonians.

- There is a sense of mourning and grief over the city's downfall.

- The chapter mentions how Judah's allies have turned against her and become her adversaries, adding to her distress.

- The chapter suggests that Jerusalem's desolation is a result of her sins and transgressions against God.

- It highlights the idea of divine punishment for disobedience.

What stands out to you in this chapter?

Where do you see God in this chapter?

How have you been challenged while reading this chapter?

Any lingering thoughts or questions following the reading?

ead Lamentations 2   **Date** _____

ecap:

- Zion's gates have fallen to the ground and are destroyed.

- Who can heal this city?

- Despite the dire situation, the people plead for God's mercy and intervention. They acknowledge their transgressions and seek forgiveness.

What stands out to you in this chapter?

Where do you see God in this chapter?

How have you been challenged while reading this chapter?

Any lingering thoughts or questions following the reading?

Read Lamentations 3   **Date** _____

Recap:

- The people are in "chains" without God.

- Souls are being deprived of peace.

- The people hope God will show compassion, according to His abundant, faithful love.

What stands out to you in this chapter?

Where do you see God in this chapter?

How have you been challenged while reading this chapter?

Any lingering thoughts or questions following the reading?

Read Lamentations 4   **Date** _____

Recap:

- The walls are broken down, and the buildings are destroyed, leaving Jerusalem in ruins.

- The glorious temple of the Lord, which was a symbol of His presence among His people, has been destroyed by the enemy.

- The prophets and priests have failed the people, preaching false messages and not seeking God's guidance. Their guilt adds to the city's downfall.

- Jerusalem's destruction is a result of her sins and rebellion against God.

- It emphasizes the importance of righteousness and obedience to God's commandments.

What stands out to you in this chapter?

Where do you see God in this chapter?

How have you been challenged while reading this chapter?

Any lingering thoughts or questions following the reading?

Read Lamentations 5   **Date** _____

Recap:

- The people express their sorrow and anguish over the destruction of Jerusalem and the desolation of its once glorious buildings.

- The people lament the heavy taxes and the oppression they face from their conquerors.

- The people express their grief over the mistreatment and abuse of widows and orphans.

- Despite the desperate situation, the chapter ends with a glimmer of hope, trusting in God's steadfast love and faithfulness.

What stands out to you in this chapter?

Where do you see God in this chapter?

How have you been challenged while reading this chapter?

Any lingering thoughts or questions following the reading?

The Book of Titus

ead Titus 1   **Date** _____

ecap:

- The letter is written by Paul to Titus, his true child in a common faith, who is left in Crete to put things in order and appoint elders in every town.

- Paul quotes a Cretan prophet, stating that Cretans are always liars, evil beasts, and lazy gluttons. This is mentioned to emphasize the need for sound teaching and leadership in Crete.

What stands out to you in this chapter?

Where do you see God in this chapter?

How have you been challenged while reading this chapter?

Any lingering thoughts or questions following the reading?

Read Titus 2   **Date** _____

Recap:

- Paul encourages Titus to teach sound doctrine and refute those who contradict it, ensuring that the church remains grounded in the truth.

- Paul reminds Titus to teach the people to live godly lives, reflecting the transformative power of the Gospel.

What stands out to you in this chapter?

Where do you see God in this chapter?

How have you been challenged while reading this chapter?

Any lingering thoughts or questions following the reading?

ead Titus 3   **Date** _____

ecap:

- Paul urges Titus to remind the believers to be submissive and obedient to rulers and authorities, to be ready for every good work.

- Paul reminds the believers that they were once foolish, disobedient, deceived, and enslaved to various passions and pleasures, living in malice and envy, hateful, and hating one another.

- Paul emphasizes that when the goodness and loving kindness of God our Savior appeared, He saved us, not because of works done by us in righteousness, but according to His own mercy.

What stands out to you in this chapter?

Where do you see God in this chapter?

How have you been challenged while reading this chapter?

Any lingering thoughts or questions following the reading?

The Book of Philemon

Read Philemon   **Date** _____

Recap:

- Paul writes on behalf of Onesimus, a slave who had become a believer while with Paul in prison.

- Paul appeals to Philemon to receive Onesimus back, not as a slave but as a beloved brother.

- Paul offers to take any debts or wrongs done by Onesimus upon himself, implying that if there is any wrongdoing or financial loss, Paul will repay it.

What stands out to you in this chapter?

Where do you see God in this chapter?

How have you been challenged while reading this chapter?

Any lingering thoughts or questions following the reading?

The Book of Joel

Read Joel 1   **Date** _____

Recap:

- Joel describes a locust invasion that has devastated the land, consuming all vegetation and leaving the fields desolate.

- Joel warns that the locust invasion is just a precursor to a more significant judgment that will come upon the land in the form of a "day of the Lord."

- Joel speaks of God's promise to restore the land and bless it abundantly once the people return to Him in genuine repentance.

What stands out to you in this chapter?

Where do you see God in this chapter?

How have you been challenged while reading this chapter?

Any lingering thoughts or questions following the reading?

Read Joel 2   **Date** _____

Recap:

- Joel describes an impending invasion of a mighty and numerous army that will bring destruction upon the land, likening it to a day of darkness and gloom.

- Joel prophecies God's response to the people's repentance.

- He will remove the threat of the invading army, drive them away into a barre and desolate place, and destroy them completely.

- Joel assures that everyone who calls on the name of the Lord shall be saved.

What stands out to you in this chapter?

Where do you see God in this chapter?

How have you been challenged while reading this chapter?

Any lingering thoughts or questions following the reading?

ead Joel 3   **Date** _____

ecap:

- Joel describes the judgment as a great harvest, with the wicked being gathered like sheaves and thrown into the winepress of God's wrath.

- Joel foretells that on that day, the mountains will drip with sweet wine, and the hills will flow with milk.

What stands out to you in this chapter?

Where do you see God in this chapter?

How have you been challenged while reading this chapter?

Any lingering thoughts or questions following the reading?

The Book of Amos

Read Amos 1   **Date** _____

Recap:

- The book of Amos begins with an introduction, identifying Amos as one of the shepherds of Tekoa.

- Amos delivers messages of judgment against various nations surrounding Israel, including Damascus (Syria), Gaza (Philistia), Tyre (Phoenicia), Edom, Ammon, and Moab. Each nation is condemned for their cruelty, aggression, and sins against God and humanity.

- Amos reveals that the Lord will not revoke His judgments, as the nations and Israel continue in their wickedness and rebellion.

What stands out to you in this chapter?

Where do you see God in this chapter?

How have you been challenged while reading this chapter?

Any lingering thoughts or questions following the reading?

ead Amos 2   **Date** _____

ecap:

- The judgment on Moab, Judah, and Israel.

- Amos condemns Israel for their oppression of the poor and needy, and for their sexual immorality.

- Amos warns that God's judgment will be swift and sure, leaving no escape for those who try to evade it.

What stands out to you in this chapter?

Where do you see God in this chapter?

How have you been challenged while reading this chapter?

Any lingering thoughts or questions following the reading?

Read Amos 3   **Date** _____

Recap:

- Amos compares the Lord's proclamation of judgment to the roaring of a lion

- Amos warns the rulers and leaders of Israel, who are oppressing the people and living in luxury while exploiting the poor and needy.

- Amos condemns those who store up violence and robbery in their palaces, predicting that their luxurious dwellings will be plundered and their riches taken away.

What stands out to you in this chapter?

Where do you see God in this chapter?

How have you been challenged while reading this chapter?

Any lingering thoughts or questions following the reading?

ead Amos 4   **Date** _____

ecap:

- Amos refers to the rich and luxurious women of Samaria as the "cows of Bashan," a region known for its fertile pastures. These women are condemned for their oppression and exploitation of the poor.

- Amos recounts various punishments that God has sent upon the people of Israel, including famine, drought, blight, locusts, pestilence, and military defeat. Despite these calamities, the people have not returned to the Lord.

- Amos rebukes the people for their insincere worship, as they bring their sacrifices and offerings with impure hearts.

What stands out to you in this chapter?

Where do you see God in this chapter?

How have you been challenged while reading this chapter?

Any lingering thoughts or questions following the reading?

Read Amos 5   **Date** _____

Recap:

- Amos laments the fallen state of Israel, saying that the virgin of Israel has fallen and will not rise again.

- Amos warns that the day of the Lord will be a day of darkness and not light, a day of judgment and not deliverance.

- Amos urges the people to seek good and not evil, to establish justice in the gates, and to hate evil and love good.

What stands out to you in this chapter?

Where do you see God in this chapter?

How have you been challenged while reading this chapter?

Any lingering thoughts or questions following the reading?

Read Amos 6   **Date** _____

Recap:

- Amos condemns the wealthy and influential people in Samaria who are living in ease and complacency while ignoring the distress and suffering of others.

- Amos prophesies that the people will be the first to go into exile, carried away as captives by foreign invaders.

- Amos calls the people to seek the Lord and live, emphasizing the importance of turning to God in genuine repentance.

What stands out to you in this chapter?

Where do you see God in this chapter?

How have you been challenged while reading this chapter?

Any lingering thoughts or questions following the reading?

Read Amos 7   **Date** _____

Recap:

- The vision of the locusts, fire, then the plumb line are a vision for Amos.

- Amos defends his prophetic calling, stating that he is not a professional prophet, but rather, God called him from his occupation as a shepherd and a tender of sycamore fruit to be His messenger.

- Amos prophesies that Amaziah's wife will become a prostitute in the city, his sons and daughters will be killed in battle, and his land will be divided and given to others.

What stands out to you in this chapter?

Where do you see God in this chapter?

How have you been challenged while reading this chapter?

Any lingering thoughts or questions following the reading?

ead Amos 8   **Date** _____

ecap:

- Amos sees a vision of a basket of ripe summer fruit, symbolizing the nearness of Israel's judgment.
- Amos condemns the religious hypocrisy of the people, particularly their eagerness to end religious festivals and Sabbaths to resume their dishonest practices of buying and selling.

What stands out to you in this chapter?

Where do you see God in this chapter?

How have you been challenged while reading this chapter?

Any lingering thoughts or questions following the reading?

Read Amos 9   **Date** _____

Recap:

- Amos sees a vision of the Lord standing by the altar, and He commands the destruction of the temple and the striking down of the tops of the pillars, so that they fall on the people.

- Despite the judgment, God declares that He will not utterly destroy the house of Jacob. He will sift the house of Israel among all nations, but not a single grain will fall to the ground.

- God promises that the days are coming when the plowman will overtake the reaper, and the mountains will drip with sweet wine.

- God promises to restore the fortunes of His people Israel, and they will rebuild the ruined cities and inhabit them.

What stands out to you in this chapter?

Where do you see God in this chapter?

How have you been challenged while reading this chapter?

Any lingering thoughts or questions following the reading?

The Book the Obadiah

ead Obadiah   **Date** _____

ecap:

- God's judgment is pronounced against Edom, and the prophecy foretells the complete destruction of the nation.

- Their allies will betray them, and their wisdom will fail.

- The prophecy concludes with the restoration of Israel's inheritance, including the regions currently occupied by Edom.

- Israel will possess the land promised to them by God.

What stands out to you in this chapter?

Where do you see God in this chapter?

How have you been challenged while reading this chapter?

Any lingering thoughts or questions following the reading?

The Book of Johan

Read Jonah 1   **Date** _____

Recap:

- Instead of obeying God's command, Jonah attempts to flee from His presenc by boarding a ship headed in the opposite direction, to Tarshish.

- The sailors, in fear of the Lord's wrath, ask Jonah what they should do to calr the storm.

- Jonah instructs the sailors to throw him into the sea, believing that it will calm the storm and save the ship and the sailors.

- The Lord provides a great fish to swallow Jonah, and he remains in the belly of the fish for three days and three nights.

What stands out to you in this chapter?

Where do you see God in this chapter?

How have you been challenged while reading this chapter?

Any lingering thoughts or questions following the reading?

ead Jonah 2   **Date** _____

ecap:

- From inside the belly of the fish, Jonah prays to the Lord, crying out to God for help.

- In his desperate situation, Jonah promises to turn back to the Lord and offer sacrifices of thanksgiving. He vows to fulfill his pledges and give praise to God.

- The fish obeys God's command, and Jonah is thrown up onto dry land.

What stands out to you in this chapter?

Where do you see God in this chapter?

How have you been challenged while reading this chapter?

Any lingering thoughts or questions following the reading?

Read Jonah 3   **Date** _____

Recap:

- This time, Jonah obeys the Lord's command and goes to Nineveh, a journey that would have taken him about three days.

- When Jonah enters the city, he proclaims a message of judgment: "Forty more days, and Nineveh will be overthrown!"

- The people of Nineveh, from the greatest to the least, believe Jonah's message.

- They declare a fast and put on sackcloth as a sign of their repentance.

What stands out to you in this chapter?

Where do you see God in this chapter?

How have you been challenged while reading this chapter?

Any lingering thoughts or questions following the reading?

ead Jonah 4   **Date** _____

ecap:

- He prays to the Lord, expressing his frustration and even wishing for death.

- God sends a worm to attack Jonah's plant, causing it to wither and die.

- God uses the situation with the plant to teach Jonah a lesson about compassion and the value of human life.

What stands out to you in this chapter?

Where do you see God in this chapter?

How have you been challenged while reading this chapter?

Any lingering thoughts or questions following the reading?

The Book of Micah

Read Micah 1   **Date** _____

Recap:

- Micah proclaims a message of judgment against both Samaria, the capital of the northern kingdom of Israel, and Jerusalem, the capital of the southern kingdom of Judah.

- He warns of their impending destruction and desolation due to their sins and idolatry.

- Micah calls the people of Judah to mourn and lament in sackcloth as a sign of their repentance and contrition.

What stands out to you in this chapter?

Where do you see God in this chapter?

How have you been challenged while reading this chapter?

Any lingering thoughts or questions following the reading?

Read Micah 2   **Date** _____

Recap:

- Micah accuses the wealthy landowners of coveting and seizing the fields and houses of the poor, leaving them homeless and destitute.

- Micah warns that because of their greed and oppression, the people will face judgment from God.

- Micah also addresses the false prophets who mislead the people by preaching messages of peace and prosperity, contrary to God's true word.

What stands out to you in this chapter?

Where do you see God in this chapter?

How have you been challenged while reading this chapter?

Any lingering thoughts or questions following the reading?

Read Micah 3   **Date** _____

Recap:

- Micah begins by addressing the rulers and leaders of Israel, denouncing their corruption and injustice.

- Micah also condemns the false prophets who lead the people astray with their deceptive messages.

- Despite the impending judgment, the rulers and prophets remain confident in their own strength and righteousness, but it will not save them from God's wrath.

What stands out to you in this chapter?

Where do you see God in this chapter?

How have you been challenged while reading this chapter?

Any lingering thoughts or questions following the reading?

ead Micah 4   **Date** _____

ecap:

- Micah describes a time of peace when nations will no longer engage in warfare, and swords will be beaten into plowshares and spears into pruning hooks.

- Micah also speaks of God's judgment on the nations that have oppressed and mistreated His people. They will be gathered and punished for their injustices.

What stands out to you in this chapter?

Where do you see God in this chapter?

How have you been challenged while reading this chapter?

Any lingering thoughts or questions following the reading?

Read Micah 5   **Date** _____

Recap:

- Micah foretells that the Messiah's reign will extend to the ends of the earth. He will bring peace and righteousness, and His rule will be far-reaching and everlasting.

- God will execute judgment on the nations and put an end to their sorceries and witchcraft.

- God will destroy all the carved images and sacred pillars, so that there will be no more idol worship among His people.

What stands out to you in this chapter?

Where do you see God in this chapter?

How have you been challenged while reading this chapter?

Any lingering thoughts or questions following the reading?

Read Micah 6   **Date** _____

Recap:

- Micah condemns the people's dishonesty and violence, describing their use of dishonest scales and deceitful weights in trade.

- Micah warns of the consequences of their sins, predicting that their land will become desolate and their cities will be laid waste.

- Micah offers hope of restoration for those who repent and turn back to the Lord.

What stands out to you in this chapter?

Where do you see God in this chapter?

How have you been challenged while reading this chapter?

Any lingering thoughts or questions following the reading?

Read Micah 7   **Date** _____

Recap:

- Micah proclaims his trust in God's salvation, acknowledging that even in dark times, God will be a light for those who follow Him.

- Despite the sins of the people, Micah declares that God is compassionate and forgiving.

- He is ready to pardon and show mercy to those who repent and turn back to Him.

What stands out to you in this chapter?

Where do you see God in this chapter?

How have you been challenged while reading this chapter?

Any lingering thoughts or questions following the reading?

The Book of Nahum

Read Nahum 1   **Date** _____

Recap:

- Nahum is stating how God is not quickly angered, but he is mighty in power and does not let guilt go unpunished.

- Nineveh is deserving of destruction.

- There is a great warning for the Assyrian king of his elimination, but a word of hope for Judah.

What stands out to you in this chapter?

Where do you see God in this chapter?

How have you been challenged while reading this chapter?

Any lingering thoughts or questions following the reading?

Read Nahum 2   **Date** _____

Recap:

- Nahum begins to describe a war against Nineveh.

- God is all powerful and will win any war how He wants.

What stands out to you in this chapter?

Where do you see God in this chapter?

How have you been challenged while reading this chapter?

Any lingering thoughts or questions following the reading?

ead Nahum 3   **Date** _____

ecap:

- Here is a description of more of what Nineveh can expect because of their idolatry.

- God is using past destruction to describe what will happen to them.

- The King of Assyria has no one ready for this battle, and no one will feel bad that this has happened to them.

What stands out to you in this chapter?

Where do you see God in this chapter?

How have you been challenged while reading this chapter?

Any lingering thoughts or questions following the reading?

The Book of Habakkuk

Read Habakkuk 1   **Date** _____

Recap:

- Habakkuk cries out to God about the injustices he sees.

- God responds by telling Habakkuk He is working in ways he won't believe that will include the Chaldeans.

- Habakkuk responds saying he doesn't believe that God would use wickedness to drive out wickedness.

What stands out to you in this chapter?

Where do you see God in this chapter?

How have you been challenged while reading this chapter?

Any lingering thoughts or questions following the reading?

fort>fort>fort>fort>3fort>fort>fort>fort>3fort>fort>fort>fort>3fort>fort>fort>fort>3fort>fort>fort>fort>3fort>fort>fort>fort>3fort>fort>fort>fort>3fort>fort>fort>fort>3

fort>fort>fort>fort>fort>fort>fort>fort>fort>fort>fort>fort>fort>

ead Habakkuk 2   **Date** _____

ecap:

- Habakkuk waits and then God responds and tells him to write down His answer.
- God warns Him that he is using the Chaldeans (Babylon) but they won't have success for themselves.
- The Chaldeans rely on false idols that will not answer them or get them anywhere.

What stands out to you in this chapter?

Where do you see God in this chapter?

How have you been challenged while reading this chapter?

Any lingering thoughts or questions following the reading?

Read Habakkuk 3   **Date** _____

Recap:

- Habakkuk's prayer begins with the awe and wonder of God.

- He shows how God can do anything.

- Habakkuk is worried about what will happen but he knows God knows wha He is doing and he can trust Him.

What stands out to you in this chapter?

Where do you see God in this chapter?

How have you been challenged while reading this chapter?

Any lingering thoughts or questions following the reading?

The Book of Zephaniah

ead Zephaniah 1   **Date** _____

ecap:

- The Lord tells Zephaniah how he will wipe everything out.

- All the things men prepare for will not be enjoyed by them.

What stands out to you in this chapter?

Where do you see God in this chapter?

How have you been challenged while reading this chapter?

Any lingering thoughts or questions following the reading?

Read Zephaniah 2   **Date** _____

Recap:

- There is a chance to be saved from the Lord's anger: seek righteousness and humility.

- No one is safe from destruction, it will all be given to Judah.

- God is avenging poor treatment of His people.

What stands out to you in this chapter?

Where do you see God in this chapter?

How have you been challenged while reading this chapter?

Any lingering thoughts or questions following the reading?

Read Zephaniah 3   **Date** _____

Recap:

- Jerusalem is called out for their disobedience and their treacherous prophets and priests.

- The Lord tells of His warnings hoping they would accept correction, but they became even more corrupt.

- God will leave the meek and humble and they will know Him.

- God saves and He loves His people. He protects them.

What stands out to you in this chapter?

Where do you see God in this chapter?

How have you been challenged while reading this chapter?

Any lingering thoughts or questions following the reading?

The Book of Haggai

Read Haggai 1   **Date** _____

Recap:

- The Lord came to Haggai and instructs him to help them see how their ways have not served them well and it is time to finish the temple.

- The people "feared the Lord" and obeyed the words of Haggai.

What stands out to you in this chapter?

Where do you see God in this chapter?

How have you been challenged while reading this chapter?

Any lingering thoughts or questions following the reading?

ead Haggai 2   **Date** _____

ecap:

- God tells them to be strong, work, and that He will be present among them to make the temple greater than ever.

- Any contact with a corpse makes something defiled, but they will not become holy by touching the temple. He will bless them though.

- God is going to rock all the rulers and leadership they know but he has chosen Zerubabel and will make him great.

What stands out to you in this chapter?

Where do you see God in this chapter?

How have you been challenged while reading this chapter?

Any lingering thoughts or questions following the reading?

ADVENT

This section is for the 25 days of December leading up to, and including, Christmas.   Begin on December 1st. We have chosen topics that will help you set your heart on why we needed a Savior and the goodness of God.   We hope you allow these verses to penetrate your heart and truly ready yourself to reflect on what this season means to your faith.

ROMISES

December 1   READ Isaiah 9:2,6,7

The people walking in darkness have seen a great light; on those living in the land
f deep darkness, a light has dawned...For to us a child is born, to us a son is given,
nd the government will be on his shoulders. And he will be called Wonderful
Counselor, Mighty God, Everlasting Father, Prince of Peace. Of the greatness of his
overnment and peace there will be no end. He will reign on David's throne and
ver his kingdom, establishing and upholding it with justice and righteousness from
hat time on and forever. The zeal of the Lord Almighty will accomplish this."
All the way back in Isaiah, 400-500 years before Jesus was born, we see God
etting the stage for Jesus to come. What a confusing and exciting prophecy!   It's
asy for us to think it's believable because we know how the story ends.   We can
ee the whole picture.   This is the perfect passage to begin to put us in the mood
or Jesus' birth.   This passage can start to soften our heart and point us toward
gratitude as we enter this season.

What things help you set your heart toward gratitude for the gift that God sent us; in
Jesus?

December 2   READ Deuteronomy 18:5

For centuries, God's people had been waiting for a Messiah. There were over 300
Old Testament passages that referenced the Messiah. These prophecies were very
specific in their details. God makes promises to His people and God keeps His
promises.

How does seeing that these prophecies were made and fulfilled help you believe
that Jesus is the true Messiah and you can follow Him?

WAITING

December 3   READ Isaiah 40:3-5

Be prepared!   Actively wait.   Actively be patient.   Be ready.   The message hasn changed.   Then they were preparing and cleansing their hearts for their Messiah the first time He came.   We prepare now for Him to come again.   We don't jus sit and wait.   We prepare our hearts.   We help others to hear about and be ready for Him.

What does actively waiting for Jesus to return mean to you?   What are you doing to make yourself ready?

December 4   READ James 1:12

This is a hard one. This life can be hard - and we don't even have the daily persecution some Christians have!   Regardless, we have trials.   The life of a Christian is not a privileged one - we have all the same hardships others can have. Luckily we have a God who we can rely on and loves us, but it can still be hard to get through this life.   We are waiting for the promise. We are waiting for that crown at the end.   That waiting can be hard.   At least we are in this together! How do you get through trials of this life?

Does the faith in the promise at the end help?

December 5   READ Isaiah 40:31

Hope in God gives us our strength to get through! It gives us the energy we need! When we rely on Him we don't grow weary.   Sometimes we get this strength straight from Him.   We go to His word, we go to Him in prayer.   Sometimes we get it from the support of other believers.   We are there to lift each other up when we can't do it for ourselves.   We are there to point each other back to TRUTH and to God.   We need each other!

How have other believers helped you sustain the hardships in life?

December 6   READ James 5:7 - 9

There's that word we all love to hear. PATIENT.   Be patient.   Sounds like fun right? The valuable thing comes after the waiting.   We know what is coming.   God's word is always true.   God has said it will happen and it will.   WE can have assurance in that.   That helps with the patience, doesn't it?   Knowing the outcome and that God has it all planned out should help us to be able to wait for it.   We can trust Him.

How has reading about God's promises and watching them happen helped you in your growth in the area of patience?

December 7   READ Psalm 27:13-14

What is your state of mind when waiting? Do you stress? Do you worry? Do you try to find little ways to take control over the situation?   These verses are showing us that our waiting time is supposed to be to our benefit. We are supposed to see God's goodness in it.   Take heart, means we are supposed to take peace, take gratitude, take joy.   In the waiting we know God is working.   His best for us is better than we could ever do or imagine for ourselves.

When have you found joy and peace in waiting?   Does this come hard for you?

December 8   READ Habakkuk 2:3
God knows everything.   Past, present, and future.   He assures us that he has it all planned to work out perfectly.   We have complete trust that nothing is a surprise nor will it ever be. If he promises it, it will happen exactly how He wants it and in His perfect time.   When we insert ourselves or try to figure it out, we are acting like we can do better than God!   Our pride is saying that God isn't good enough to handle it - he needs our help!   How dare we think that we could work out the details better than the one who created the universe!

How have you acted like you could do something better than God?

How can you involve God more in your actions and give up more control to Him?

December 9   READ Revelation 22:20

The last few verses of the Bible. Yes, I am coming soon. Soon is relative though, right? It's already been centuries since this was said. But are you ready? Are you ready to say "Come, Lord Jesus"? When we trust in Jesus and repent of our sins, we have confidence that we don't have to worry about eternity, but don't we worry about eternity for our friends and family around us? This is such as sobering reality and the point of this Advent devotion when we say "don't wait!" Do not wait and think you are guaranteed a tomorrow when Jesus says he is coming soon! There should be urgency in making sure you have told all those you love about Jesus and the salvation he has to offer. What they do with that is up to them and God, but we should be in a rush to make sure they know! Don't wait!

Make a list of your friends and family that you need to make sure have heard about Jesus from you! What are you waiting for! Make a date with them today!

PEACE

December 10   READ Matthew 2:9-1?

These Magi - wise men - knew what they were searching for when they headed ou
to follow the star.   What an experience!   They had all been waiting for a Messia
and these men knew he had been born.   They couldn't wait to worship Him.   The
even put themselves in danger with Herod to do it!   What an experience!

Allow yourself to imagine the joy and excitement the Magi would have felt coming
to meet the baby Messiah.
Write out what you think it would have been like.

December 11   READ Numbers 6:22-27
This is one of my favorite blessings in the Bible.   Just the thought - the first real
priest given instructions by God of what to pray over the people.   His promise to
love them and keep them and be gracious to them.   His promise to give them
peace.   What a beautiful way to bless the people.   The privilege Aaron had to be
a part of it.   The way God just loves His people and wants the best for Him over
and over.
Read this blessing every day this week and allow your soul to soak it in.   These
words are for all of God's people.   That's you.

When you read these words, what feelings come up?   How does this change your
outlook?

December 12   READ Matthew 5:9

Part of the Sermon on the Mount, the Beatitudes, Jesus calls out those who strive to make peace.   There's a big difference between peacekeepers and peacemakers.   I think Jesus talks about the peacemaking side intentionally.   PeaceMAKERS do the hard work or working things out to create peace.   They don't just try to keep the peace by not ruffling feathers and tiptoeing around issues.   Peacemakers do the hard work or work through issues so all are at peace.

Where have you made the decision to be a peacemaker instead of a peacekeeper?
How have you seen this done well?

December 13   READ 2 Thessalonians 3:16

What a way to end a letter, right?   May God give you peace in every way at all times!   How does that happen?   You have to walk real close with him in order for His peace to be with you and not leave you.   Doesn't that sound amazing?   Think of how your life could be if you lived that reality.   Think of how much more content and joyous you could be.   Well this is for you too! You can have this! As you spend more and more time talking with God, walking closely with Him, letting him into every area of your life, His peace rubs off on you!   He is ready and waiting to fill you with that peace.

How have you seen His peace in your life as you've grown in your relationship with Him?
How would you tell others that they can obtain that peace?

December 14   READ Colossians 2:12-17

Let the peace of Christ rule in your hearts.   What does that mean?   I think it tells us in the beginning of this section.   When you have compassion, kindness, humility, gentleness and patience, you find peace.   More importantly, when you have forgiveness and love you have peace. As you grow in each of these areas, you grow closer and more like Christ.   When you are more like him, you have more o His peace.   Doesn't that sound wonderful?

What characteristics on this list do you need to grow more in? What things can you do to put action behind that?

December 15   READ Colossians 3:13

Yes, we read this yesterday.   But we need to focus more on this verse in the section.   Forgiveness, We all have big feelings about this word.   It's one of those things that we want others to give us easily but it is so hard for us to give. With God, forgiveness isn't a suggestion.   Forgiveness is something we are called to do as representatives of Him.   He has forgiven us for EVERYTHING we have done. What is so important that someone has done to us that we can't find it in us to forgive them? It is hard, but it also helps us grow.   When we are obedient to God's commands, we grow closer to Him.   Obedience is easier next time.
Bear with each other and forgive one another if any of you has a grievance against someone.

When has it been hard to forgive but you did it?   How did you feel after?

December 16   READ Hebrews 12:14-17

Make every effort to live at peace with everyone.   See to it that no one falls short of grace.   See to all these things.   Being in community is a huge aspect of our walk with God.   He didn't design for us to do life alone.   He actually gives us warnings of our responsibility to each other.   We do better together.   But this is a big responsibility.   We have to be vulnerable with each other and allow them to hold us accountable.   We have to be willing to say hard truths to each other when necessary.   We have to hold each other to God's standard.   But We have to be at peace so we have to do it in love with the best intentions.

How has living in community helped you grow closer to God?   How has it helped you stay away from sin?

ADORATION

December 17   READ John 3:16-21

Wow. That sums it up. Everything God has done for us. He has saved the world through His Son. We are innately evil and gravitate toward darkness, but He steps in and gives us access to the light.   Could anything else deserve more adoration? Sometimes it's easy to get bogged down with daily life and checking off the boxes of what we think we need to do as Christians.   In reality we need to spend more and more time in adoration of what He has done for us!

Spend time making a list of all the reasons God deserves your gratitude.
Who he is and all the things he's done for you.

December 18   READ Psalm 95

Everything about God deserves our adoration.   He deserves to be approached as a father and friend.   He deserves to be worshiped as a great King.   That dynamic can be hard for people.   We are able to come to Him with everything at any time, but we have to keep in mind His magnificence and majestic nature.   One of the ways we can keep this balance is to actually bow down in worship and kneel before Him when we come to Him in prayer.

Try that today.   When you spend time with Him, fall to your knees and start your time by worshiping HIm.
How did this time feel different?

December 19   READ Deuteronomy 10:12-22

God chose you! Allow his love and goodness to penetrate your heart. He is great
and mighty and awesome and he CHOSE YOU. He stands up for the orphans and
widows. He cares for those that flee their home. God is SO amazingly big and yet
he is so loving and caring for the little guy. He is both. God blesses His people.
He grew them greatly. He blesses us too.

How has God's love for others influenced your love for others as you've grown
closer to Him?
Does seeing how he loves the marginalized make you want to do more?

December 20   READ 1 Samuel 2:1-11

Not everything God does looks good to us. He sees the big picture. The whole
plan. How it all works together to bring people to Him. What may look like an
unanswered prayer or a NO to what we have asked, may actually be what's best for
us. It's our job to trust Him and his plan. It's our job to worship and adore Him
even in the waiting or the NO times.

When has God said NO to a prayer that you prayed but you saw later that it worked
out better than you could imagine?

December 21   READ Revelation 5:11-14

Can you imagine! All the angels praising God.   All the creatures everywhere on earth and under earth worship Him.   Every knee will bow eventually.   Every living thing will know who God is. Aren't you glad you know who He is NOW and don' realize it when it's too late?   You have the chance to honor and worship God with your life while you are still living on earth.   That's a big job, but it's also such a privilege.   You get the chance to live your life in a God honoring way!

How do you live your daily life to honor God?
What things could you do to better live a life of worship?

December 22   READ Isaiah 6

I love to read these verses and see the respect that Isaiah had for God.   He is living through a magnificent moment and his biggest fear is that he saw God and isn't worthy of it! But when God asks who he should send to do His work, he instantly volunteers! He loves God so much he would do anything to be used by Him and to serve Him!

When was the last time that you said to God "Here I am Lord, use Me!"?
How do you set your heart to know what God is asking you to do?

December 23   READ 2 Chronicles 6:12-42

Solomon begins his dedication of the temple with worship of God. This is good for his heart to set his sights on all the good things of God, but it also helps all those in the crowd. A big part of the dedication is Solomon recognizing how God has always kept His promises to them. He is showing them that God has done it before so they can trust He will do it again. He has no doubt. Solomon continues on in humility showing how he doesn't feel worthy that God will dwell with them on earth in the temple that was built. But he did. He wants to be with His people.

How has God shown you that He is with you?
What past things has He done that help you believe he will be with you in the future?

Christmas Eve

December 24   READ Luke 1:26 - 56

What a startling event that happened to Mary!   Mary is graceful and faithful in he
response! I love the reminder here "Nothing is impossible with God."   Mary
clearly believed it!   Elizabeth believed it!   John the Baptist - from the womb -
believed it! Mary's praise and understanding of who God is is so inspiring.
Imagine the judgment and gossip she had to face.   An engaged girl in the
community all the sudden is pregnant.   How could they not read into that?
Imagine her relationship and how hard it would have been to explain and face.
Yet, she praises God and is so willing to carry this burden because she has faith an
believes that what the angel told her was true.   She is carrying the SAVIOR of the
WORLD!

How do you think you would have reacted in Mary's shoes?

How do you think her faith remained so strong?

Spend time in gratitude to God for this amazing gift to the world he has given.

Christmas Day

December 25   READ Luke 2:1-21

What a beautiful picture this paints.   The angels encouraging everyone with "good news with great joy!"   And then a multitude coming and saying "Glory to God in the highest, and on earth peace among those with whom he is pleased!"   Imagine this experience!   No wonder the shepherds wanted to make the trek to see what was going on.   Mary was treasuring up this whole experience.   She pondered them in her heart.   Can you imagine!   What a boost for your faith.   To be told about the Messiah by a multitude of angels.   To go and see Him with their own eyes.   Of course they were glorifying and praising God!   I imagine they couldn't contain themselves from telling everyone around them this Truth!   I wonder how infections their excitement was.   How did it encourage those in their lives?   This should still be the case for us today!   Today we remember that God sent our Savior to be born!   Today is the day we celebrate that that happened.   The day that changed all our lives - changed the world!   Let yourself feel that excitement today and celebrate!

Is your excitement today pouring out to those around you?

Do they see what an impact the birth of Jesus has on you and your life?

Reflect and see why or why not this may be the case for you.

Allow yourself to celebrate!

LENT

This section is for the 47 days leading up to Easter. Begin on Ash Wednesday (dates vary year to year so consult any calendar for the exact date). We have chosen topics that to remind us of God's goodness for each week to help set your heart on the impact that the life of Jesus had on the world.   The few days leading up to Easter more closely examines the events occurring during the crucifixion and resurrection to set the tone for your Easter celebration.   We pray that, in reading this, your Easter celebrations are more meaningful and you are better able to share your faith.

ALVATION

ay 1 - Ash Wednesday

EAD Acts 2:36-40   Date _____

hey realized they were responsible for the death of the REAL SON of God.   This roke their heart.   They were devastated.   But there was another chance for them. or us.   Repent.   Be baptized.   You will be forgiven.   You will get the Holy Spirit! his promise isn't just for them.   It's for you.   It's for everyone.

xamine your heart as you begin this Lent journey.
How have you been grieved by the crucifixion of the Savior?
How has your repentance and filling of the Holy Spirit changed your life?

Day 2
READ John 14:5-14   Date _____

Sometimes we tend to try to make our own ways to get to the Father.   WE try to earn our way by being good enough or doing enough of the right things.   Working for it.   Jesus tells us all here that the only way we can ever reach the Father is through Him.   This goes back to the "REPENT and be BAPTIZED " that we read yesterday.   It can be so hard to leave it at that and not try to take control of the relationship.

How have you fallen into the trap of trying to get to the Father by your own means?
What has helped you to let go of that control?

Day 3
READ Ephesians 2:1-10   Date _____

Our fleshly desires are the opposite of everything God is about.   We have selfish
desires and thoughts, we deserve nothing but wrath.   But God.   He steps in and
gives us all the love and mercy and a new life.   We are made new!   It is the FRE
gift of God!

How does it make you feel to read about who you were before God reached into
your heart and made it new?
How does this help you relate to those in your life that are unsaved?

Day 4
READ Acts 16:23-34   Date _____

Don't you feel such a sense of urgency here?   Paul and Silas gave the jailer such a
great gift when they remained in their jail cell.   They saved his life.   He knew there
was something different about them immediately and was receptive to what they
had to say about salvation.   He immediately accepted it and was baptized.   Not
only him but his whole household!

We have such great influence on those around us.   More than we realize.
Especially on those that live in our own homes or those we do life with.

How have you seen the truth in this?   How can you better reflect this in the way
you live?

GOD'S PROMISES

Day 5
READ Ephesians 3:14-21/Isaiah 41:10   Date _____

God promises us strength.
We often feel powerless and weak up against the trials of this life.   We can get
beaten down and feel like there's no hope.   God promises that when we come to
Him, trust in Him, follow His plan, we will be strengthened.   He will inherit His
strength for the battle.   The more we grow our trust in Him, the easier our trials
become.

How has your strength in God grown over your time knowing Him?
How has this strength helped you in your trials?

Day 6
READ Matthew 11:25-30   Date _____

God promises to give you rest.
Do you ever feel weary and burdened from all the things of this life?   Do you ever
feel like you can't get deep rest?   Doesn't this passage sound wonderful?   Rest.
Deep soul rest.   That's what we need and it's what He has to offer us.   Come to
Him.   Yoke yourself with Him.   His ways are the best ways.   Give up control to
Him.   The more we grow in our knowledge and closeness of the Lord, the more
His ways become our ways and the more His peace becomes our peace.   He
promises rest.

In what areas do you still need to give up your ways, your control, and yoke
yourself to Him?
Where have you had success in trusting Him in this and what has been the
outcome?

Day 7
READ Matthew 7:7-12/Proverbs 1:23-33   Date _____

God promises to answer your prayers.
God hears us when we pray.   Sometimes is it easy to forget that?   He knows
before we even come to Him what is in our hearts.   God isn't a genie but he loves
us and wants to take care of us.   Is this saying we will get everything we ask for?
Nope.   God sees the BIG picture.   He wants us to be taken care of and be able to
fully rely on him.   If what we are asking for doesn't align our hearts more toward
Him or won't help us show His glory, it's not something we really need in our lives.
He knows these things better than we do.   As we grow in our relationship and
know Him more, our hearts naturally align with Him and our wants change to be
things that he would want for us too.   He promises to answer those prayers.

How have you seen your "needs" and "wants" change as you've grown closer to
God?
How do you work to align your heart more like His?

Day 8
READ Joshua 1:1-6/Matthew 28:19-10   Date _____

God promises to be with you.
You never have to face anything in this life by yourself.   As we see in Joshua, God
has promised to always be with His people.   As we see in Matthew, Jesus promises
to be with you forever.   We have the Holy Spirit at all times.   We tend to forget this
and take everything on as if we are doing it by ourselves. We need to call on God
to take charge when things get hard.   He's ready and waiting for us to allow Him to
comfort and guide us.   We don't have to go through this life alone, but we have to
let Him lead.   He promises to be with us.

How has God shown you that He is with you in the hard times?
How do you let Him lead you in these times?

Day 9
READ John 5:16-30   Date _____

God promises you everlasting life.
No matter what we face in this life, we have eternity with God to look forward to.
Nothing can take that away from you.   When we remember this, it is a lot easier
to get through the grind of daily life.   Not only is this promise to live forever, but all
evil will be gone.   All sin will be gone.   Only beauty and love will remain.
God promises us that we will live forever with Him.

What are you most looking forward to in your days living with God?

Day 10
READ Psalm 91:1-16   Date _____

God promises to protect you.
God is FOR you.   He wants the best for you.   He wants you to win every battle.
When you call on Him, He can make the enemy flee.   He will not let the enemy
harm you, but you need to allow Him to be that refuge and protection for you.   So
many times we go into our days - our battles - unarmed, army-less.   When we
allow Him, He promises to protect us.

What hard lessons have you had to learn before allowing God to be your refuge in
times of trouble?

Day 11
READ Romans 8:31-39   Date _____

God promises that nothing can separate you from Him.
When you have repented and been forgiven, absolutely NOTHING can separate
you from the love of Christ!   You are HIS and HE is YOURS.   Isn't that a
wonderful thought?   Anything this world throws at you….   Anything you think o
do….   Nothing can take away Christ's love from you.   As you rest in this truth, le
yourself feel the gratitude that comes.   He has promised that NOTHING can
separate you from Him.

How does it make you feel to know that nothing can separate you from His love?
What action does this push you toward?

CONFESSION

Day 12
READ James 5:13-20   Date _____

Confession is important to our salvation.   James is saying that confession in our community is very important too.   It is important to help keep us on track.   Our community is vital to our faith and we tend to forget that.   We need to be accountable to each other and humble enough to confess our sins to each other so that we can stay on track in our relationship with the Lord.   He uses those in our community to help us.

How has your community been a helpful aspect to growing your faith?
Do you confess your sins to your community often?

Day 13
READ 1 John 1:5-10   Date _____

Why do we think we can hide our sins from God?   Do we not think he knows our heart and sees our plans before we even do them?   As we grow in our sanctification, we grow in humility.   Our sin grieves us more and more and we confess more easily because we want to be cleansed of the things that separate us from Him.   Our goal is to be totally transparent and let Him mold our hearts to look more like Him.
How have you seen growth in your willingness to confess your sin?

Day 14
READ Proverbs 28   Date _____

We are kept from God's mercy when we hide our sin.   Sin separates us from Him.
God wants nothing more than to cleanse us of our guilt and shame but until we are
willing to come to Him and confess it, we cannot have that peace.   As we hold on
to sin, our hearts harden and we refuse to realize who God truly is.   Freedom
comes with owning the sin in our lives and giving it to Him.   He is ready and
waiting to take it.

How do you respond to those that think they are too sinful or are living with too
much guilt and shame to come to God?
How has His mercy set you free?

Day 15
READ Leviticus 5:2-6   Date _____

Yes this is the Old Testament.   Sometimes it's good to see the difference in how
Israel had to live and how we live now as Christ followers.   I, for one, am so
grateful for His salvation and that I am no longer called to offer sacrifices for each
time I mess up.   There were so many small laws to keep every day that it could be
easy to mess up - and you might not even know you did!   We sin every day.
Maybe we don't steal or murder, but we might tell a little white lie or think thoughts
that God says are "like murder".   Since we don't have a list in front of us of all the
ways we sin, it can be easy to think we are "doing good" or we haven't sinned.
Jesus covers all those sins, but we need to be aware that we do it.   Jesus takes
away all our guilt and shame but we have to go to him and ask for it.

Write a short prayer of gratitude for your freedom from sacrificial law as well as
shame and guilt.

ay 16
EAD Acts 3:11-26   Date _____

eter is calling for the repentance of the descendants of Israel for crucifying Jesus.
hey are astonished by his miracles but still deny the miracles of Jesus.   We
annot be saved until we acknowledge the sin we have done and the sin in our
earts.   God sees it all whether we try to hide it or don't even realize it's there.
Ie is ready and waiting to show you what is keeping you   from the fulness you can
ave in him, but repentance is key to it all.

pend time in prayer asking the Spirit to search your heart and bring to light hidden
in.   Then repent and turn from those things.
Iow has God made you aware of hidden sin in the past?

Day 17
READ James 4:1-12   Date _____

Purified hearts are the longing of every believer.   Are we putting effort into that
happening?   God is ready and willing to be with us and change us, but we have to
act first.   We have to approach him in humility and ask.   He doesn't make us do
anything - we want us to be willing participants that desire closeness with Him.

How do you put effort into drawing near to God and allowing Him to purify your
heart?

Day 18
READ Mark 1:1-8   Date _____

Even before Jesus was crucified, died, and rose from the dead, John the Baptist knew that confessions were an integral part of a believer's life.   He knew one was coming that would forgive the sins of those who believed and he wanted them ready.   Many believed and were baptized.

How can you help others see the need for repenting and being baptized? What has your repentance done for you?

REPENTANCE

Day 19
READ Acts 3: 17-26   Date _____

Yes, we just read this part of Acts.   But there's a layer to the confession that we
haven't examined yet.   That's the REPENTANCE part.   The TURN BACK part.
When we confess our sins we are acknowledging that we have sin in our life.
When we add the repentance layer, that means that we turn from it.   We go
forward doing the opposite of what we were doing.

How often have you confessed a sin and then continued on in it a few days later?
It can be hard to change behavior, but true repentance requires it.
Allow the Spirit time to show you ways to truly repent for the sins going on in your
life.

Day 20
READ 2 Peter 3:1-13   Date _____

God WANTS to give you time to get it right..   He wants to be patient and merciful
toward you no matter your actions.   The thing we have to remember is that we
don't know how much time we have.   We waste so much time living in our sin
and thinking we will work to change it later.   Why make life on this earth harder
than it has to be?   Turn away from those sins that are keeping you from living in the
fullness that you could with God.

As you have grown in your relationship with God, how have your feelings about
your sin changed?
How do you take it more seriously as you mature?
What helps you turn from sin patterns?

Day 21
READ 2 Chronicles 7: 11-22

Date _____

Have you ever thought about how God forgives our sins but we keep on doing the same thing?   When we read about Israel and the ways they keep disobeying God, we can see how God just wants what's best for them.   If they'd only turn from their sin, He has so much better for them.   He can't move forward with those plans until their hearts change and they truly turn from their sinful patterns they are living in.   Have you thought about how that could be the same in your life?   God has so many amazing ways He can use us.   He has so many plans to incorporate us and let us in on the big things he's doing - but is our sin getting in the way of that?

Make a list (with the Spirit's help) of sins that could be inhibiting you from fully being used by God.
Pick one sin and write some ways that you could work to get that specific sin out of your life for good.

Day 22
READ Matthew 3:1-12   Date _____

bear fruit in keeping with repentance.   Prove by the way you live that you have
repented of your sins and turned to God.   People around you are watching.   I'm
not talking about the judgmental - waiting for you to mess up like some people in
society are doing as they watch Christians go about their lives.   I'm talking about
your friends, your family, your co-workers….   That person you invited to church….
They are all watching.   They are seeing if your actions - your fruit - matches with
what you say.   Are you flashing sinful behaviors for the world to see?   Are you
showing that you are ok with sin being a pattern of your life?   OR do you sin, but
show that you are remorseful.   DO you go out of your way to show that you are
putting in effort to move past certain sins that they may see?

How have you seen a Christian in your life be "OK" with their sin and not show
any remorse or public repentance?
How have you seen a Christian in your life model the fact that they are human but
are actively working against sin patterns?

Day 23
READ Luke 15:1-7   Date _____

God knows we will always have sin.   We will be fighting it until the day we die.
It is the heart condition we show that He is looking forward to.   Does your sin
grieve you?   Are you continually repenting and putting in the effort to change that
behavior?   Are you implanting the strategies to conquer it or are you hiding/
denying it?   Every time we depend, He rejoices.   Think of that as you work
toward conquering sin - God rejoices over your work!   What a thought!

Record a time that you have conquered a bigger sin in your life and how it felt.
Did you feel like rejoicing? Did you feel like God was rejoicing with you?

Day 24
READ 2 Corinthians 7:2-16   Date _____

Can you remember a time when you felt shame or guilt for your actions? You maybe even sometimes do now.   Paul is showing us the joy that we can have in th Lord.   When we sin and repent, we can let it go.   God looks at us as if it never happened.   What a relief is that!? God is so good!

How have you moved from shame and guilt in your life to the JOY of the Lord? If you or someone you know are having a hard time getting there, what things could help you?

Day 25
READ Ezekiel 18: 19-32   Date _____

Just like we cannot be saved on the faith of our fathers and mothers, God does not hold us to any actions other than our own.   We are not held accountable for our parent's actions, but we are held accountable for our own.   God takes delight in every single heart that turns toward Him. There is no one too wicked, no action too awful for God to not be ready and waiting to show mercy.   When we repent, God is fair and just and offers salvation.

What would you say to someone who thinks they are too far gone for God to want to save them?

FORGIVENESS

Day 26
READ Colossians 3:1-17   Date _____

When you become a believer and repent of your sins, you are not only forgiven, but you become NEW. Born again.   It's a clean fresh start.   That means you need to cleanse your heart of unforgiveness. How can you have a clean heart that has room for all the things God wants to fill it with, if you are dwelling on something someone has done to you?   We need to actively work to give up those parts that hold unforgiveness so God can fully cleanse you and you can grow into the person he always knew you'd be.   Every little bit of unforgiveness keeps that part of your heart from being fully His and inhibits your relationship with Him.

In what ways has your heart been made new, when you chose to accept Christ's gift of salvation?

Day 27
READ Luke 23: 26-43   Date _____

Can you imagine caring for someone's soul to the point that as they beat and murder you, you pray for God to take it easy on them? That is why Jesus is Jesus and I am not! His heart was so very pure, but he is still a good example to us.   If he can care so deeply that they are forgiven, how can we hold small offenses against those that we know?   Is anything done to you ever as huge as this?   This isn't easy, but it's definitely something that we should be aiming for!

How can you begin to look at those around you - especially those you may call enemies - more like God sees them?

Day 28
Ephesians 4:17-32   Date _____

Paul is writing a letter to the church at Ephesus.   He is telling them how to relate to each other.   You would think that other brothers and sisters in the church would be the ones you'd have to forgive.   BUT, when you live closely and do so many things together, you don't always see eye to eye.   Feelings get hurt. Kindness may not be at the forefront.   We all fall into worrying about our own self interests.   Paul is telling us all in the church to give each other the benefit of the doubt.   Assume the best in each other.   When something does happen, be quick to forgive.   Nothing will split a church like harboring unforgiveness.

How have you seen the church flourish but being quick to forgive and assuming the best in each other?
How have you seen this go wrong?

Day 29
READ Mark 11:20-26   Date _____

This is a very important warning that every Christian needs to take to heart.   If you have unforgiveness, it inhibits your relationship with God.   Your prayer life is one of your most important connections to God and when you are refusing to allow forgiveness to happen, your prayer life suffers.   You can't fully be connected to God when you are dwelling on these things.   We tend to think that forgiveness is about the other person, but in reality, forgiveness is between us and God.   When we clear out the unforgiveness we are fully about to give our hearts over.

How have you felt held back in your relationship with God?
How has working through forgiveness helped?

Day 30
READ Matthew 18: 21-35   Date _____

Do you ever really sit and think and allow yourself to fill with gratitude over the fact that God has forgiven you and no longer sees you as the sinful person you once were? It's out of that gratitude that we are expected to be able to forgive the things that have been done to us.   The only way we can move into that grace that has been given to us is to leave all that behind.   Move forward. We have to trust that God only has the best in mind for us and he knows better than we do.   We get nowhere by harboring those bad feelings.   We have to move on and the only way to put it all behind us is to make the decision to forgive.

Allow the Spirit time to examine your heart and list any unforgiveness that comes to mind.   Take steps to talk with God and move into forgiveness on those issues.

Day 31
READ Proverbs 17: 9-15   Date _____

When we grow in our relationship with God, we aim to show all the Fruit of the Spirit.   Among them are love, peace, and kindness.   When we are quick to forgive an offense, we promote relationships and friendship with those around us.   When we aren't, we separate and feed into hostility. That is not the picture that God wants us to present to those around us.   We are to be a representation of His character, and what better way than to let things go quickly!

How have you gotten better at letting things go quickly as you've grown in your faith?
What has helped you?

Day 32
READ Matthew 6:9-15   Date _____

The Lord's Prayer
This is the model prayer that Jesus told all believers to pray.   We can't just skip
over a major section.   Forgive us our trespasses - forgive us our sins - as we have
forgiven those that sinned against us.   He is telling us to ask God to treat us as we
have already treated others!   What if He really did that??   How would He be
treating you right now?   Would He be holding your sins against you?   Would He
be giving you the cold shoulder?   Would He be holding hatred in his heart?
Luckily we know God shows us mercy, but Jesus is calling us to do better.   If we
expect God to treat us with love and grace, who are we to not offer that to others?

Pray the Lord's prayer in your quest time this week.
Take this section to heart and ask Him to help you really live out these words.

RUST

Day 33
READ Psalm 56:1-13   Date _____

David is being pursued by his enemies.   He isn't saying he isn't afraid or feeling like it's not OK to be afraid, but he also knows who God is.   He knows his character and that no matter what, he can trust that God has him under his protection.   He can get through this because God is on his side.   Men are nothing in comparison to the greatness of God.

How has God shown you he can be trusted when you are fearful of what comes next?

Day 34
READ Isaiah 26:1-6   Date _____

God is a rock, He is always there and always steady.   When you set your mind on Him in times of trial, He gives you peace because he is so trustworthy.   It seems weird to those who don't believe, but there are many times where Christians have reported being in dangerous, chaotic situations, but felt at perfect peace because they know that God is with them.   He can be trusted.

When have you been at peace when the world would say you should be frazzled and anxious?

Day 35
READ Matthew 6:25-34   Date _____

God cares about the little things in your life.   God cares about the big things in
your life.   He knows you need food and clothing and he will make sure you have
those needs met.   He doesn't want us to spend our days worrying.   He wants us to
trust Him - that he will make things work out.   Spending your time worrying only
takes your focus off of Him and what he has for you to be doing while you're on
earth.

As you've grown to know him better, what steps do you take to not worry and let
Him carry out His plan?

Day 36
READ Jeremiah 17:7-8   Date _____

When God is the source of your strength, you will have nothing to worry about.
You will go through life saying YES to the things he asks of you and you will be
stronger and more joyous because of it.   You will find your peace in the things of
God and you will see the people around you as He sees them.   You won't feel the
need to take matters into your own hands.   Can you imagine the daily peace of
being fully rooted and fed by the spring that is God?

Have you known someone that is this fully dependent and trusting of God?   What
made them different?

ay 37
EAD 2 Samuel 7: 18 - 29   Date _____

We know God is trustworthy because of His track record.   We can depend on His
word because of the ways He has said he'd do it and followed through in the past.
This is why it is so important to keep a record of the things God has done for you
in the past.   During hard times, you can go back through and see all that He has
done for you. God made David a promise and he has NO doubt that He will carry
: out.   Don't you want to have full confidence that God will do everything He says
He will do for you?

Make a log of some of the major things that you've seen God do in your life.
How does this help you trust Him in the future?

Day 38
READ Romans 15:1-13   Date _____

As you grow in your trust of God, you also grow in your joy and peace.   They go
hand in hand.   You don't get His peace and joy automatically.   You can become a
believer and still be grumpy and mad.   You can not let the Spirit fill you or trust
that God is who He says He is.   Look at everything that person is missing out on!
The JOY and PEACE that we grow to have as our trust in Him grows is so so good!
Make sure you aren't missing out!

How has your joy and peace grown as your trust in God has grown?
How would you explain this to a new believer?

Day 39
READ 1 Thessalonians 2:1-16   Date _____

This is a different take on trust.   This is God trusting US.   It is our job to share the Gospel so more people around us know Him.   He is trusting that we will get it right.   That it will keep its integrity as we tell people about it.   He is trusting that won't be watered down or misrepresented.   That's a big job we have!   We want to make sure the people we tell about Christ come away knowing the magnitude of what He is offering!   That they fully understand why they need Him and what it means to accept His gift.

When was the last time you got to share the Gospel with someone?
How was it shared with you?

SANCTIFICATION

Day 40
READ 2 Thessalonians 2:13-17

Date _____

Do you even look around at your brothers and sisters in Christ and give thanks to God for the work He's done in them? Give thanks that you get to be part of a big family together? We spend a lot of time complaining about what we don't have, or even just focusing on ourselves. We can be so encouraged by the sanctifying work that God does in the people around us! When we notice what God is doing, it can be easier to see what he does in/for us, too!

Look around at the brothers and sisters you do life with.
Who have you seen growth in recently?
Send them a quick text of encouragement that you see the Spirit's work in them!

Day 41
READ Colossians 3:1-17

Date _____

We see a list like this and think "of course we don't carry these earthly things as Christians." Then we get to the second list. Anger. When did you last deal with that? Malice? When was the last time you thought someone deserved something bad to happen to them? Have you told a little white lie recently? The point is, these are the things we are actively working to put away. As the Spirit works in you, you become more like the image of the creator. You have more from the list of compassion, kindness, humility, meekness, and patience. It helps to see where you've come from and where you are now to encourage you to keep growing into that new self.

Examine your history with sin.
What things do you find you don't deal with anymore?
What things from the "good" list have you obtained in your New Life?
Praise God for his visible work in your life!

Day 42
READ Galatians 2:15-21   Date _____

Christ lives in me and I live by faith in Jesus!   We can't WORK our way to
sanctification.   It is not something we EARN.   It is something we allow to happen
to us through our faith and trust and through practices that help us grow in our
relationship with God.   As we grow closer to Him, we more easily hear the
prompting of the Spirit which allows us to more freely grow and change our heart
toward Him.   He does all the work, but we have to allow the changes to happen.
We have to be willing participants!

What practices have you implemented in your faith journey to grow in your
relationship with God?
Praise God for His accessibility through the Spirit!

Day 43
READ Hebrews 10:1-18   Date _____
Christ is the only one that could take away sins.   The Law had so many rules and
people had to sacrifice animals, but that couldn't fully take away their sins.   He
came to die for our sins.   By doing that, he was doing God's will.   By His doing
God's will, we are sanctified.   He was perfect and we will be made perfect one
day.   We are in the process of becoming more and more holy here on earth, but
until we are with Him forever, we will not be made perfect like Him.   As long as
sin is involved, we will never be fully Holy.

Spend today really dwelling on what God sent Jesus to do for his people.   As we
have spent time in the Old Testament, we have seen all the ways humans have
messed up God's gift over time.   We see how we all mess up His gift now.   He
made a new way for us to be made perfect to spend eternity with Him.   Talk to
Him about what that means to you!

MAUNDY THURSDAY

Day 44
READ Matthew 26   Date _____

SO MUCH happens in this one chapter.   You begin with a warning from Jesus himself of what is to come. You get a glimpse behind the scenes of what the priests and elders were thinking as they plotted out Jesus' death. They were worried they'd cause a riot!   But that didn't stop them!   Jesus knew what was to come, but he still had work to do.   Plans to carry out. One of my favorite take-aways from these verses is that Jesus took time to fellowship and commune with people and with God on this chaotic day.   First we see him reclining in the house of Simon the leper.   Getting anointed with perfume. Teaching lessons. Next we see him eating with his disciples. Spending time with those important to Him. Teaching lessons.   His work is never finished.   He uses up every last minute. After this, He goes with his disciples to have time with God away from everything else in a garden. We see his agony but also his willingness to do God's will.   Thursday is one of the most important days in the story of our salvation.   We see many great teachings of Jesus, we see Him teaching about communion, we see Him accept what has to happen, and we see things he said would happen come to pass.

What importance does Maundy Thursday have on your faith?

What new insights have you noticed today that help you set your heart on gratitude over the next few days?

GOOD FRIDAY

Day 45
READ John 18:28 -19:42   Date _____

How quickly things escalate.   In the morning, Jesus is handed over to Pilate.
Pilate didn't know what to do with him, so he passed the decision to the crowd.
The crowd is so worked up that they chose to kill Jesus and release Barabbas - a
robber!   In that instant, Jesus' fate was sealed. (I mean, God already planned it.).
Jesus was beaten and mocked. The crowd couldn't wait to see him murdered. We
see Pilate's change of heart, but it was too late. He couldn't be seen as a traitor.
Pilate still took the change to write KING OF THE JEWS on his cross.   It makes you
wonder if he had truly repented and believed in his heart at this point?   One of my
very favorite parts of this day's events is Jesus' care for His mother.   He wanted to
make sure she had community - that she was taken care of.   As he was hanging on
the cross, He cared for those He loved. And with that, we see Jesus die. The worst
and the (almost) most important moment of our faith.   Gut wrenching to read
about, but also so invigorating as we see prophecy unfold.   Our God has a plan for
our salvation.   Our God loves us so much he would go to these great lengths for
us to believe it's true.   Our God is so good even in the hard.
What feelings does this reading bring up?
Are you wrestling with anger, sadness, gratitude and overwhelming love too?
It's OK to have all the feelings and not really know what to do with them.   It
makes this day all the more important and special that it invokes so many strong
feelings.

Take this day to feel these feelings.   Be sure as it comes up, to tell those around
you about this bid day in your faith!

SATURDAY

READ Luke 23:54-56   Date _____

Today is Sabbath.   The most important person to these early Christians has died and they still make room for a day of rest. We see Jesus model rest all throughout His ministry.   As we wait in anticipation (because we know what tomorrow holds!), take time to reflect on what the early believers would have been feeling on this day.   They gave up their lives to follow Jesus.   They spent the recent past following Him, working for Him, telling others about Him.   They saw Him brutally murdered yesterday.   Now they rest.   Together.   Community had to be so important during this time.

What do you think this Sabbath looked like for these believers?

Be sure to make time for rest today so you can fully reflect on what has happened and what is coming.

EASTER!

READ John 20   Date _____

HE IS RISEN!!
Now THIS is the most important day as a Christian!
Can you feel the sadness and confusion that turns to unbelief and then excitement?
Imagine the joy that Mary felt when Jesus said her name! Imagine her urgency to get to all her friends and family and tell them what she has seen! Jesus made sure to physically present himself to each of His disciples. They each got to see that he wasn't dead, but alive. They each got to spend time with him and not have doubt that it was true. I love the care he took with Thomas to make sure his doubts were squashed. Jesus sees each one of us and our needs. The final words say it all….
"These are written so that you may believe that Jesus is the Christ, the Son of God, and that by believing you may have life in his name."

Because of Him we now have LIFE!

How much gratitude does this invoke in you??

Do you want to run like Mary and tell everyone what your Jesus has done?

Find a way to make sure your friends and family close to you know what Jesus has done today.

Made in the USA
Las Vegas, NV
15 August 2023

76098914R00188